Francis F

John Fletcher

The Chances

Elibron Classics
www.elibron.com

Elibron Classics series.

© 2007 Adamant Media Corporation.

ISBN 1-4021-4751-1 (paperback)
ISBN 1-4212-7698-4 (hardcover)

This Elibron Classics Replica Edition is an unabridged facsimile
of the edition published in 1791 by John Bell, London.

BRIT[...]ATRE

The CHANCES.

Don John. Offer once more in another World:
this Wench cure you must appropose for me,
she is bewitched or worse humour

Smirke pinx.t   Heath sc.

London. Printed for J. Bell British Library, Strand 2ᵈ July 1791.

DeWilde ad viv. pinxt.   Thornthwaite sc.

Mr. PALMER as DON JOHN.
'Come, good wonder,
Let you and I be jogging; your star'd treble
Will waken the rude watch else.

London. Printed for J. Bell. British Library. Strand. July 2. 1791.

THE

CHANCES.

A

COMEDY.

As ALTERED FROM

BEAUMONT AND FLETCHER,

BY HIS GRACE

THE DUKE OF BUCKINGHAM.

ADAPTED FOR

THEATRICAL REPRESENTATION,

AS PERFORMED AT THE

THEATRES-ROYAL,

DRURY-LANE AND COVENT-GARDEN.

REGULATED FROM THE PROMPT-BOOKS,

By Permission of the Managers.

" The Lines distinguished by inverted Commas, are omitted in the Representation.'

LONDON:

Printed for the Proprietors, under the Direction of
JOHN BELL, British Library, STRAND,
Bookseller to His Royal Highness the Prince of Wales.
M DCC XCI.

THE CHANCES.

This pleasing Comedy is built upon a beautiful Tale, to be found in the Novelas Exemplares of the inimitable Cervantes ; though the Play is certainly much inferior to the Novel. Indeed the admirable Spaniard is beyond any competition, except that of Shakspere.—Ingenious in the structure of his Tales, they abound in various incidents well combined, in profound observation of life, in acute perception of character. Working from such materials, a good Dramatist could not go far wrong. —Beaumont and Fletcher have never succeeded better in their comic skill.—The Soliloquy in the First Act by Don John, upon perceiving his prize, is replete with ludicrous images.

A lover of the sterling excellence of our early Bards will frequently regret the mutilated state, in which, for something or for nothing, their best plays are performed upon our Stages.—If the plea held out for such arbitrary alteration were at all founded, and the critic pruning knife abscinded those gross impurities, which our fastidious age bears rather the commission of than the mention, something might be gained; but the fact is totally otherwise—these ble-

mishes are ever suffered to remain, as in the Piece
before us, and what we lose is too frequently the
glorious exuberance of comic expression lowered
down to the imperfect organs of a capricious Actor,
who, in the vanity of his heart, hates every sentence
that cannot be cut into a set of hemistic clap-traps.

GARRICK, to the disgrace of his Theatre, in-
fluenced by the insipidities of French criticism, mutilated HAMLET thus, and impaired the noblest mo-
nument of genius that the world possesses.—The
people, who are never deluded long, restored as
much of their favourite as was possible then; and
more NOW ought to follow.—This is no beginning
age of literature; we have pretty generally discri-
minative powers—let us therefore discriminate for
OURSELVES.

PROLOGUE.

OF all men, those have reason least to care
For being laugh'd at, who can laugh their share :
And that's a thing our author's apt to use,
Upon occasion, when no man can choose.
Suppose now at this instant one of you
Were tickled by a fool, what would you do ?
'Tis ten to one you'd laugh: here's just the case,
For there are fools that tickle with their face.
Your gay fool tickles with his dress and motions,
But your grave fool of fools with silly notions.
Is it not then unjust that fops should still
Force one to laugh, and then take laughing ill ?
Yet since perhaps to some it gives offence,
That men are tickled at the want of sense;
Our author thinks he takes the readiest way
To shew all he has laugh'd at here—fair play.
For if ill writing be a folly thought,
Correcting ill is sure a greater fault.
Then, gallants, laugh; but choose the right place first,
For judging ill is of all faults the worst.

Dramatis Personae.

DRURY-LANE.

Men.

DUKE of FERRARA, - -	- Mr. Packer.
PETRUCHIO, *Governor of* Bologna,	- Mr. Aickin.
Don JOHN, ⎱ *two* Spanish *gentle-*	⎰ Mr. Palmer.
Don FREDERICK, ⎰ *men and comrades.*	⎱ Mr. Barrymore.
ANTONIO, *an old stout gentleman, kins-*	
man to Petruchio, - -	- Mr. Parsons.
Three Gentlemen, *friends to the* Duke,	-
Three Gentlemen, *friends to* Petruchio,	-
FRANCISCO, - - - -	- Mr. Chaplin.
Musician, - - - -	- Mr. Spencer.
Antonio's Boy, - - - -	- Mr. Alfred.
PETER, *and* ⎱ *two servants to Don* John	⎰ Mr. Burton.
ANTHONY, ⎰ *and* Frederick,	⎱ Mr. Phillimore.
Surgeon, - - - -	- Mr. Jones.

Women.

1st CONSTANTIA, *sister to* Petruchio, *and*	
mistress to the Duke, - -	- Mrs. Ward.
Kinswoman, - - - -	- Miss Barnes.
Landlady *to Don* John *and* Frederick,	- Mrs. Love,
2d CONSTANTIA, *whore to* Antonio,	- Miss Farren.
Bawd, - - - - -	- Mrs. Booth.
Mother-in-law, - - -	- Mrs. Hopkins.

Dramatis Personae.

COVENT-GARDEN.

Men.

DUKE of FERRARA, - - -	Mr. Davies.
PETRUCHIO, *Governor of* Bologna, -	Mr. Macready.
Don JOHN, } *two* Spanish *gentle-* {	Mr. Harley.
Don FREDERICK, } *men and comrades,* {	Mr. Marshall.
ANTONIO, *an old stout gentleman, kins-*	
man to Petruchio, - - -	Mr. Quick.
Three Gentlemen, *friends to the* Duke, -	
Three Gentlemen, *friends to* Petruchio, -	
FRANCISCO, - - - - -	
Musician, - - - - -	
Antonio's Boy, - - - -	Mr. Rock.
PETER, *and* } *two servants to Don* John {	Mr. Blanchard.
ANTHONY, } *and* Frederick, {	Mr. Cubitt.
Surgeon, - - - - - -	Mr. Powell.

Women.

1st CONSTANTIA, *sister to* Petruchio, *and*	
mistress to the Duke, - - -	Miss Chapman.
Kinswoman, - - - - -	Mrs. Platt.
Landlady *to Don* John *and* Frederick, -	Mrs. Pitt.
2d CONSTANTIA, *whore to* Antonio, -	Mrs. Pope.
Bawd, - - - - - -	
Mother-in-law, - - - -	Mrs. Webb.

THE

CHANCES.

ACT I. SCENE I.

Enter PETER *and* ANTHONY, *two Serving-men.*

Peter.

WOULD we were remov'd from this town, Anthony,
That we might taste some quiet; for mine own part,
I'm almost melted with continual trotting
After enquiries, dreams and revelations,
Of who knows whom or where. Serve wenching sol-
      diers!
I'll serve a priest in Lent first, and eat bell-ropes.

  Ant. Thou art the forwardest fool—

  Pet. Why, good tame Anthony,
Tell me but this; to what end came we hither?

  Ant. To wait upon our masters.

  Pet. But how, Anthony?
Answer me that; resolve me there, good Anthony.

  Ant. To serve their uses.

B

Pet. Shew your uses, Anthony.

Ant. To be employ'd in any thing.

Pet. No, Anthony,

Not any thing, I take it, nor that thing
We travel to discover, like new islands;
A salt itch serve such uses! in things of moment,
Concerning things I grant ye, not things errant,
Sweet ladies' things, and things to thank the surgeon:
In no such things, sweet Anthony.   Put case——

    Ant. Come, come, all will be mended: this invi-
       sible woman,

Of infinite report for shape and beauty,
That bred all this trouble to no purpose,
They are determin'd now no more to think on.

    Pet. Were there ever

Men known to run mad with report before?
Or wander after what they know not where
To find; or if found, how to enjoy?   Are men's
    brains
Made now-a-days with malt, that their affeƈtions
Are never sober; but like drunken people
Pounder at every new fame? I do believe
That men in love are ever drunk, as drunken men
Are ever loving.

    Ant. Pr'ythee, be thou sober,

And know that they are none of those, not guilty
Of the least vanity of love: only a doubt
Fame might too far report, or rather flatter
The graces of this woman, made them curious
To find the truth; which since they find so

Lock'd up from their searches, they are now resolv'd
To give the wonder over.

Pet. Would they were resolv'd
To give me some new shoes too; for I'll be sworn
These are e'en worn out to the reasonable soles
In their good worship's business: and some sleep
Would not do much amiss, unless they mean
To make a bell-man of me.　Here they come.

> [*Exeunt.*

Enter Don JOHN *and Don* FREDERICK.

John. I would we could have seen her tho': for sure
She must be some rare creature, or report lies:
All men's reports too.

Fred. I could well wish I had seen Constantia:
But since she is so conceal'd, plac'd where
No knowledge can come near her, so guarded
As 'twere impossible, tho' known, to reach her,
I have made up my belief.

John. Hang me from this hour,
If I more think upon her;
But as she came a strange report unto me,
So the next fame shall lose her.

Fred. 'Tis the next way—
But whither are you walking?

John. My old round,
After my meat, and then to bed.

Fred. 'Tis healthful.

John. Will you not stir?

Fred. I have a little business.

John. I'd lay my life, this lady still——
Fred. Then you would lose it.
John. Pray let's walk together.
Fred. Now I cannot.
John. I have something to impart
Fred. An hour hence
I will not miss to meet ye.
John. Where?
Fred. I' th' high street :
For, not to lie, I have a few devotions
To do first, then I'm yours.
John. Remember.   [*Exeunt.*

Enter PETRUCHIO, ANTONIO, *and two gentlemen.*

Ant. Cut his wind-pipe, I say.
1 *Gent.* Fie, Antonio.
Ant. Or knock his brains out first, and then for-
     give him.
If you do thrust, be sure it be to th' hilts,
A surgeon may see through him.
    1 *Gent.* You are too violent.
    2 *Gent.* Too open, indiscreet.
    Petr. Am I not ruin'd?
The honour of my house crack'd? my blood poison'd?
My credit and my name?
    2 *Gent.* Be sure it be so,
Before you use this violence. Let not doubt
And a suspecting anger so much sway ye,
Your wisdom may be question'd.
    Ant. I say, kill him,

And then dispute the cause; cut off what may be,
And what is shall be safe.

   2 *Gent.* Hang up a true man,
Because 'tis possible he may be thievish :
Alas! is this good justice ?

   Petr. I know as certain
As day must come again, as clear as truth,
And open as belief can lay it to me,
That I am basely wrong'd, wrong'd above recom-
      pence,
Maliciously abus'd, blasted for ever
In name and honour, lost to all remembrance,
But what is smear'd and shameful: I must kill him,
Necessity compels me.

   1 *Gent.* But think better.

   Petr. There's no other cure left; yet witness with me
All that is fair in man, all that is noble;
I am not greedy for this life I seek for,
Nor thirst to shed 'man's blood; and would 'twere
      possible,
I wish it with my soul, so much I tremble
T' offend the sacred image of my Maker,
My sword should only kill his crimes : no, 'tis
Honour, honour, my noble friends, that idol honour,
That all the world now worships, not Petruchio,
Must do this justice.

   Ant. Let it once be done,
And 'tis no matter, whether you or honour,
Or both, be accessary.

   2 *Gent.* Do you weigh, Petruchio,

The value of the person, power, and greatness,
And what this spark may kindle?

 Petr. To perform it,
So much I am tied to reputation,
And credit of my house, let it raise wild-fires,
And storms that toss me into everlasting ruin,
Yet I must through; if ye dare side me.

 Ant. Dare!

 Petr. Y' are friends indeed : if not!

 2 Gent. Here's none flies from you;
Do it in what design you please, we'll back ye.

 1 Gent. Is the cause so mortal? nothing but his life?

 Petr. Believe me,
A less offence has been the desolation
Of a whole name.

 1 Gent. No other way to purge it?

 Petr. There is, but never to be hop'd for.

 2 Gent. Think an hour more,
And if then you find no safer road to guide ye,
We'll set our rests too.

 Ant. Mine's up already,
And hang him, for my part, goes less than life.

 2 Gent. If we see noble cause, 'tis like our swords
May be as free and forward as your words. [*Exeunt.*

Enter *Don* JOHN.

 John. The civil order of this city Naples
Makes it belov'd and honour'd of all travellers,
As a most safe retirement in all troubles;
Beside the wholesome seat and noble temper
Of those minds that inhabit it, safely wise,

And to all strangers courteous.   But I see
My admiration has drawn night upon me,
And longer to expect my friend may pull me
Into suspicion of too late a stirrer,
Which all good governments are jealous of.
I'll home, and think at liberty : yet certain,
'Tis not so far night, as I thought ; for see,
A fair house yet stands open, yet all about it
Are close, and no lights stirring ; there may be foul
     play :
I'll venture to look in.   If there be knaves,
I may do a good office.

   Within. Signior!
   John. What! How is this ?
   Within. Signior Fabritio !
   John. I'll go nearer.
   Within. Fabritio !
   John. This is a woman's tongue ; here may be good
     done.
   Within. Who's there ? Fabritio ?
   John. Ay.
   Within. Where are you ?
   John. Here.
   Within. O, come for heaven's sake !
   John. I must see what this means.

      Enter a Woman with a Child.

   Wom. I have stay'd this long hour for you ; make
     no noise ;
For things are in strange trouble.   Here, be secret.

'Tis worth your care: begone now; more eyes
    watch us
Than may be for our safeties.

    John. Hark ye.

    Wom. Peace; good night.

    John. She's gone, and I am loaden. Fortune for me!
It weighs well, and it feels well; it may chance
To be some pack of worth: by th' mass 'tis heavy!
If it be coin or jewels, it is worth welcome.
I'll ne'er refuse a fortune; I am confident
'Tis of no common price. Now to my lodging:
If it be right, I'll bless this night.   [*Exit.*

Enter Don FREDERICK.

    Fred. 'Tis strange,
I cannot meet him; sure he has encounter'd
Some light o' love or other, and there means
To play at in and in for this night. Well, Don John,
If you do spring a leak, or get an itch,
Till you claw off your curl'd pate, thank your night-
    walks;
You must be still a boot-haling. One round more,
Tho' it be late, I'll venture to discover ye;
I do not like your out-leaps.   [*Exit.*

Enter DUKE *and three Gentlemen.*

    Duke. Welcome to town. Are ye all fit?

    1 *Gent.* To point, sir.

    Duke. Where are the horses?

    2 *Gent.* Where they were appointed.

Duke. Be private ; and whatsoever .fortune
Offer itself, let us stand sure.

3 *Gent.* Fear us not.
Ere you shall be endanger'd or deluded,
We'll make a black night on't.

Duke. No more, I know it ;
You know your quarters.

1 *Gent.* Will you go alone, sir?

Duke. Ye shall not be far from me, the least noise
Shall bring ye to my rescue.

2 *Gent.* We are counsell'd. [*Exeunt.*

Enter Don JOHN.

John. Was ever man so paid for being curious?
Ever so bobb'd for searching out adventures,
As I am? Did the devil lead me? Must I needs be
    peeping
Into men's houses where I had no business,
And make myself a mischief? 'Tis well carry'd!
I must take other men's occasions on me,
And be I know not whom: most finely handled!
What have I got by this now? What's the purchase?
A piece of evening arras-work, a child,
Indeed an infidel! This comes of peeping!
A lump got out of laziness! Good white bread,
Let's have no bawling with ye. 'Sdeath, have I
Known wenches thus long, all the ways of wenches,
Their snares and subtleties? Have I read over
All their school learning, div'd into their quiddits,
And am I now bumfiddled with a bastard?

Fetch'd over with a card o'five, and in my old days,
After the dire massacre of a million
Of maidenheads, caught the common way, i' th'
          night too
Under another's name, to make the matter
Carry more weight about it? Well, Don John,
You will be wiser one day, when ye've purchas'd
A bevy of those butter prints together,
With searching out conceal'd iniquities,
Without commission. Why it would never grieve me,
If I had got this gingerbread : never stirr'd me,
So I had had a stroke for it : 't had been justice
Then to have kept it ; but to raise a dairy,
For other men's adultery, consume myself in caudles,
And scouring work, in nurses, bells, and babies,
Only for charity, for mere I thank you,
A little troubles me : the least touch for it,
Had but my breeches got it, it had contented me.
Whose e'er it is, sure it had a wealthy mother,
For 'tis well cloth'd, and if I be not cozen'd,
Well lin'd within.   To leave it here were barbarous,
And ten to one would kill it ; a worse sin
Than his that got it.   Well, I will dispose on't,
And keep it as they keep death's heads in rings,
To cry *memento* to me—no more peeping.
Now all the danger is to qualify
The good old gentlewoman at whose house we live ;
For she will fall upon me with a catechism
Of four hours long : I must endure all ;
For I will know this mother.   Come, good wonder,

Let you and I be jogging ; your starved treble
Will waken the rude watch else.   All that be
Curious night-walkers, may they find my fee. [*Exit.*

Enter Don FREDERICK.

Fred. Sure he's gone home :
I have beaten all the purlieus,
But cannot bolt him : If he be a bobbing,
'Tis not my care can cure him : to-morrow morning
I shall have further knowledge from a surgeon,
Where he lies moor'd to mend his leaks.

Enter 1st CONSTANTIA.

Con. I am ready :
And through a world of dangers am flown to ye.
Be full of haste and care, we are undone else.
Where are your people ? Which way must we travel ?
For Heaven's sake stay not here, sir.

Fred. What may this prove ?

Con. Alas ! I am mistaken, lost, undone,
For ever perished ! Sir, for Heaven's sake, tell me,
Are ye a gentleman ?

Fred. I am.

Con. Of this place ?

Fred. No, born in Spain.

Con. As ever you lov'd honour,
As ever your desires may gain their end,
Do a poor wretched woman but this benefit,
For I'm forc'd to trust ye.

Fred. Y' have charm'd me,

Humanity and honour bids me help ye:
And if I fail your trust——
   Con. The time's too dangerous
To stay your protestations : I believe ye,
Alas ! I must believe ye. From this place,
Good, noble sir, remove me instantly.
And for a time, where nothing but yourself,
And honest conversation may come near me,
In some secure place settle me. What I am,
And why thus boldly I commit my credit
Into a stranger's hand, the fear and dangers
That force me to this wild course, at more leisure
I shall reveal unto you.
   Fred. Come, be hearty,
'He must strike through my life that takes you from
      me.   [*Exeunt.*

Enter PETRUCHIO, ANTONIO, *and two Gentlemen.*

   Petr. He will sure come : are ye all well arm'd ?
   Ant. Never fear us :
Here's that will make 'em dance without a fiddle.
   Petr. We are to look for no weak foes, my friends,
Nor unadvised ones.
   Ant. Best gamesters make the best play ;
We shall fight close and home then.
   1 *Gent.* Antonio,
You are thought too bloody.
   Ant. Why ? All physicians,
And penny almanacks, allow the opening
Of veins this month. Why do you talk of bloody ?

What come we for ? to fall to cuffs for apples ?
What, would you make the cause a cudgel-quarrel ?
  Petr. Speak softly, gentle cousin.
  Ant. I will speak truly.
What should men do, ally'd to these disgraces,
Lick o'er his enemy, sit down and dance him ?—
  2 *Gent.* You are as far o' th' bow-hand now.
  Ant. And cry,
That's my fine boy, thou wilt do so no more, child ?
  Petr. Here are no such cold pities.
  Ant. By St. Jaques,
They shall not find me one ! Here's old tough An-
      drew,
A special friend of mine, and he but hold,
I'll strike them such a hornpipe! Knocks I come for,
And the best blood I light on : I profess it,
Not to scare costermongers. If I lose my own,
My audit's lost, and farewell five and fifty.
  Petr. Let's talk no longer. Place yourselves with
      silence
As I directed ye; and when time calls us,
As ye are friends, to shew yourselves.
  Ant. So be it.   [*Exeunt.*

Enter Don JOHN *and his Landlady.*

  Land. Nay, son, if this be your regard—
  John. Good mother—
  Land. Good me no goods—Your cousin and yourself
Are welcome to me, whilst you bear yourselves
Like honest and true gentlemen. Bring hither
                C

To my house, that have ever been reputed
A gentlewoman of a decent and a fair carriage,
And so behaved myself——

 John. I know you have.

 Land. Bring hither, as I say, to make my name
Stink in my neighbour's nostrils, your devices,
Your brats got out of alligant and broken oaths,
Your linsey-woolsey work, your hasty-puddings!
I foster up your filch'd iniquities!
You're deceiv'd in me, sir, I am none
Of those receivers.

 John. Have I not sworn unto you,
'Tis none of mine, and shew'd you how I found it?

 Land. Ye found an easy fool that let you get it.

 John. Will you hear me?

 Land. Oaths! what care you for oaths to gain your
   ends;
When ye are high and pamper'd? What saint know
   ye?
Or what religion, but your purpos'd lewdness,
Is to be look'd for of ye? Nay, I will tell ye—
You will then swear like accus'd cut-purses,
As far off truth too; and lie beyond all falconers:
I'm sick to see this dealing.

 John. Heaven forbid, mother.

 Land. Nay, I am very sick.

 John. Who waits there?

 Pet. [*Within.*] Sir!

 John. Bring down the bottle of Canary wine.

 Land. Exceeding sick, Heaven help me!

John. Haste ye, sirrah.

I must e'en make her drunk. [*Aside.*]   Nay, gentle
    mother—

Land. Now fie upon ye! was it for this purpose

You fetch'd your evening walks for your devotions?

For this pretended holiness? No weather,

Not before day, could hold you from the matins.

Where these you bo-peep prayers? Y'ave pray'd well,

And with a learned zeal have watch'd well too; your
    saint

It seems was pleas'd as well.   Still sicker, sicker!

Enter PETER *with a bottle of wine.*

John. There is no talking to her till I have drench'd
    her,

Give me. Here, mother, take a good round draught.

It will purge spleen from your spirits: deeper, mo-
    ther.

Land. Aye, aye, son; you imagine this will mend all.

John. All, i'faith, mother.

Land. I confess the wine

Will do his part.

    John. I'll pledge ye.

    Land. But, son John——

    John. I know your meaning, mother, touch it once
    more.

Alas! you look not well, take a round draught,

It warms the blood well, and restores the colour,

And then we'll talk at large.
                C ij

Land. A civil gentleman!

A stranger! one the town holds a good regard of!

John. Nay, I will silence thee there.

Land. One that should weigh his fair name!—Oh,
a stitch!

John. There's nothing better for a stitch, good mother,

Make no spare of it as you love your health;

Mince not the matter.

Land. As I said, a gentleman

Lodger'd in my house! Now Heaven's my comfort,
Signior!

John. I look'd for this.

Land. I did not think you would have us'd me thus;

A woman of my credit, one, Heaven knows,

That loves you but too tenderly.

John. Dear mother,

I ever found your kindness, and acknowledge it.

Land. No, no, I am a fool to counsel ye. Where's
the infant?

Come, let's see your workmanship.

John. None of mine, mother:

But there 'tis, and a lusty one.

Land. Heaven bless thee,

Thou hadst a hasty making; but the best is,

'Tis many a good man's fortune. As I live,

Your own eyes, Signior; and the nether lip

As like ye, as ye had spit it.

John. I am glad on't.

Land. Bless me! what things are these?

John. I thought my labour
Was not all lost; 'tis gold, and these are jewels,
Both rich and right I hope.

    Land. Well, well, son John,
I see ye're a woodman, and can choose
Your deer, tho' it be i' th' dark; all your discretion
Is not yet lost; this was well clapp'd aboard;
Here I am with ye now, when as they say,
Your pleasure comes with profit; when you must
      needs do,
Do where you may be done to; 'tis a wisdom
Becomes a young man well: be sure of one thing,
Lose not your labour and your time together;
It seasons of a fool, son; time is precious,
Work wary whilst you have it. Since you must traffic
Sometimes this slippery way, take sure hold, Signior;
Trade with no broken merchants; make your lading
As you would make your rest, adventurously,
But with advantage ever.

    John. All this time, mother,
The child wants looking to, wants meat and nurses.

    Land. Now blessing o' thy heart, it shall have all;
And instantly I'll seek a nurse myself, son.
'Tis a sweet child—Ah, my young Spaniard!
Take you no further care, sir.

    John. Yes, of these jewels,
I must by your good leave, mother; these are yours,
To make your care the stronger; for the rest,
I'll find a master; the gold for bringing up on't,
I freely render to your charge.

C iij

Land. No more words,
Nor no more children, good son, as you love me :
This may do well.

John. I shall observe your morals.
But where's Don Frederick, mother ?

Land. Ten to one,
About the like adventure ; he told me,
He was to find you out.

John. Why should he stay thus ?
There may be some ill chance in't : sleep I will not,
Before I have found him. Now this woman's pleas'd,
I'll seek my friend out, and my care is eas'd. [*Exeunt.*

Enter DUKE *and three Gentlemen.*

1 *Gent.* Believe, sir, 'tis as possible to do it,
As to move the city : the main faction
Swarm thro' the streets like hornets, and with augurs
Able to ruin states, no safety left us,
Nor means to die like men, if instantly
You draw not back again.

Duke. May he be drawn,
And quarter'd too, that turns now ; were I surer
Of death than thou art of thy fears, and with death
More than those fears are too——

1 *Gent.* Sir, I fear not.

Duke. I would not break my vow, start from my
honour,
Because I may find danger ; wound my soul
To keep my body safe.

1 *Gent.* I speak not, sir,
Out of a baseness to ye.
  Duke. No, nor do not
Out of a baseness leave me.   What is danger
More than the weakness of our apprehensions?
A poor cold part o'th' blood.   Who takes it hold of?
Cowards and wicked livers: valiant minds
Were made masters of it: and as hearty seamen
In desperate storms stem with a little rudder
The tumbling ruins of the ocean;
So with their cause and swords do they do dangers.
Say we were sure to die all in this venture,
As I am confident against it; is there any
Amongst us of so fat a sense, so pamper'd,
Would choose luxuriously to lie a-bed,
And purge away his spirits; send his soul out
In sugar-sops and syrups? Give me dying
As dying ought to be, upon mine enemy;
Parting with mankind, by a man that's manly:
Let them be all the world, and bring along
Cain's envy with them, I will on.
  2 *Gent.* You may, sir,
But with what safety?
  1 *Gent.* Since 'tis come to dying,
You shall perceive, sir, that here be those amongst us
Can die as decently as other men,
And with as little ceremony.   On, brave sir.
  Duke. That's spoken heartily.
  1 *Gent.* And he that flinches,
May he die lousy in a ditch.

Duke. No more dying,

There's no such danger in't.   What's o'clock?

3 *Gent.* Somewhat above your hour.

Duke. Away then quickly,

Make no noise, and no trouble will attend us. [*Exeunt.*

Enter FREDERICK *and* ANTHONY *with a candle.*

Fred. Give me the candle; so, go you out that way.

Ant. What have we now to do?

Fred. And on your life, sirrah,

Let none come near the door without my knowledge;

No, not my landlady, nor my friend.

Ant. 'Tis done, sir,

Fred. Nor any serious business that concerns me.

Ant. Is the wind there again?

Fred. Begone.

Ant. I am, sir.   [*Exit.*

Fred. Now enter without fear——

Enter 1st CONSTANTIA *with a jewel.*

And, noble lady,

That safety and civility ye wish for

Shall truly here attend you: no rude tongue

Nor rough behaviour knows this place; no wishes,

Beyond the moderation of a man,

Dare enter here.   Your own desires and innocence,

Join'd to my vow'd obedience, shall protect ye.

Con. Ye are truly noble,

And worth a woman's trust: let it become me,

(I do beseech you, sir) for all your kindness,

To render with my thanks this worthless trifle—
I may be longer troublesome.
   Fred. Fair offices
Are still their own rewards : heavens bless me, lady,
From selling civil courtesies. May it please ye,
If ye will force a favour to oblige me,
Draw but that cloud aside, to satisfy me
For what good angel I am engag'd.
   Con. It shall be ;
For I am truly confident ye are honest.
The piece is scarce worth looking on.
   Fred. Trust me,
The abstract of all beauty, soul of sweetness !
Defend me, honest thoughts, I shall grow wild else.
What eyes are there ! rather what little heavens,
To stir men's contemplation ! What a Paradise
Runs thro' each part she has ! Good blood, be tem-
     perate!
I must look off : too excellent an object
Confounds the sense that sees it. Noble lady,
If there be any further service to cast on me,
Let it be worth my life, so much I honour ye,
Or the engagements of whole families.
   Con. Your service is too liberal, worthy sir.
Thus far I shall entreat—
   Fred. Command me, lady :
You may make your power too poor.
   Con. That presently,
With all convenient haste, you will retire
Unto the street you found me in.

Fred. 'Tis done.

Con. There if you find a gentleman oppress'd
With force and violence, do a man's office,
And draw your sword to rescue him.

Fred. He's safe,
Be what he will; and let his foes be devils,
Arm'd with your beauty, I shall conjure them.
Retire, this key will guide ye: all things necessary
Are there before ye.

 Con. All my prayers go with ye.   [*Exit.*

 Fred. Ye clap on proof upon me. Men say, gold
Does all, engages all, works thro' all dangers:
Now I say, beauty can do more. The king's ex-
  chequer,
Nor all his wealthy Indies, could not draw me
Thro' half those miseries this piece of pleasure
Might make me leap into: we are all like sea-charts,
All our endeavours and our motions
(As they do to the north) still point at beauty,
Still at the fairest; for a handsome woman,
(Setting my soul aside) it should go hard
But I will strain my body; yet to her,
Unless it be her own free gratitude,
Hopes, ye shall die, and thou, tongue, rot within me,
Ere I infringe my faith. Now to my rescue. [*Exit.*

ACT II. SCENE I.

Enter DUKE, *pursued by* PETRUCHIO, ANTONIO, *and that faction.*

Duke.

You will not all oppress me ?

Ant. Kill him i'th' wanton eye :
Let me come to him.

Duke. Then you shall buy me dearly.

Petr. Say you so, sir ?

Ant. I say, cut his wezand, spoil his peeping:
Have at your love-sick heart, sir.

Enter Don JOHN.

John. Sure 'tis fighting !
My friend may be engaged. Fie, gentlemen,
This is unmanly odds.

> [*Duke falls ;* Don John *bestrides him.*

Ant. I'll stop your mouth, sir.

John. Nay, then have at thee freely.
There's a plumb, sir, to satisfy your longing.

Petr. Away; I hope I have sped him: here comes
rescue.
We shall be endanger'd. Where's Antonio ?

Ant. I must have one thrust more, sir.

John. Come up to me.

Ant. A mischief confound your fingers.

Petr. How is it ?

Ant. Well :
He'as given me my *quietus est* ; I felt him
In my small guts ; I'm sure he's feez'd me ;
This comes of siding with you.

    2 *Gent.* Can you go, sir?

    Ant. I shall go, man, and my head were off;
Never talk of going.

    Petr. Come, all shall be well then.
I hear more rescue coming.   [*Trampling within.*

Enter the DUKE's faction.

    Ant. Let's turn back then ;
My skull's uncloven yet, let me kill.

    Petr. Away for heaven's sake with him.
                          [*Exit cum suis.*

    John. How is it?

    Duke. Well, sir,
Only a little stagger'd.

    Duke's fact. Let's pursue them.

    Duke. No, not a man, I charge ye.   Thanks good
           coat,
Thou hast sav'd me a shrew'd welcome : 'twas put
           home,
With a good mind too, I'm sure on't.

    John. Are you safe then?

    Duke. My thanks to you, brave sir, whose timely
           valour,
And manly courtesy came to my rescue.

    John. Ye had foul play offer'd ye, and shame befal him
That can pass by oppression.

Duke. May I crave, sir,
But this much honour more, to know your name,
And him I am so bound to ?

John. For the bond, sir,
'Tis every good man's tie : to know me further,
Will little profit you; I am a stranger,
My country Spain, my name Don John, a gentleman
That came abroad to travel.

Duke. I have heard, sir,
Much worthy mention of ye, yet I find
Fame short of what ye are.

John. You are pleas'd, sir,
To express your courtesy : may I demand
As freely what you are, and what mischance
Cast you into this danger ?

Duke. For this present
I must desire your pardon : you shall know me
Ere it be long, sir, and nobler thanks,
Than now my will can render.

John. Your will's your own, sir.

Duke. What is't you look for, sir ? Have you lost
　　any thing ?

John. Only my hat i' th' scuffle ; sure these fellows
Were night-snaps.

Duke. No, believe me, sir : pray use mine,
For 'twill be hard to find your own now.

John. No, sir.

Duke. Indeed you shall, I can command another :
I do beseech you honour me.

D

John. Well, sir, then I will,
And so I'll take my leave.

Duke. Within these few days
I hope I shall be happy in your knowledge,
Till when I love your memory.   [*Exit cum suis.*

Enter FREDERICK.

John. I'm yours.
This is some noble fellow !

Fred. 'Tis his tongue sure.
Don John !

John. Don Frederick !

Fred. Y' are fairly met, sir !
I thought ye had been a bat-fowling. Pr'ythee tell me
What revelation hast thou had to-night,
That home was never thought on ?

John. Revelations !
I'll tell thee, Frederick : but before I tell thee,
Settle thy understanding.

Fred. 'Tis prepar'd, sir.

John. Why then mark what shall follow:
This night, Frederick, this bawdy night—

Fred. I thought no less.

John. This blind night,
What dost thou think I have got?

Fred. The pox, it may be.

John. Would 'twere no worse: ye talk of revela-
         tions,
I have got a revelation will reveal me
An errant coxcomb whilst I live.

Fred. What is't ?

Thou hast lost nothing?

    John. No, I have got, I tell thee.

    Fred. What hast thou got ?

    John. One of the infantry, a child.

    Fred. How !

    John. A chopping child, man.

    Fred. Give you joy, sir.

    John. A lump of lewdness, Frederick ; that's the
       truth on't,

This town's abominable.

    Fred. I still told ye, John,

Your whoring must come home ; I counsell'd ye :

But where no grace is—

    John. 'Tis none of mine, man.

    Fred. Answer the parish so.

    John. Cheated in troth

(Peeping into a house) by whom I know not,

Nor where to find the place again ; no, Frederick,

'Tis no poor one,

That's my best comfort, for't has brought about it

Enough to make it man.

    Fred. Where is't ?

    John. At home.

    Fred. A saving voyage ; but what will you say,
       signior,

To him that searching out your serious worship,

Has met a strange fortune ?

    John. How, good Frederick ?

A militant girl to this boy would hit it.

Fred. No, mine's a nobler venture : what do you
    think, sir,
Of a distressed lady, one whose beauty
Would over-sell all Italy ?

John. Where is she ?—

Fred. A woman of that rare behaviour,
So qualify'd, as admiration
Dwells round about her ; of that perfect spirit—

John. Ay marry, sir.

Fred. That admirable carriage,
That sweetness in discourse ; young as the morning,
Her blushes staining his.

John. But where's this creature ?
Shew me but that.

Fred. That's all one, she's forth-coming.
I have her sure, boy.

John. Hark ye, Frederick ;
What truck betwixt my infant ?

Fred. 'Tis too light, sir ;
Stick to your charge, good Don John, I am well.

John. But is there such a wench ?

Fred. First tell me this ;
Did you not lately, as you walk'd along,
Discover people that were arm'd, and likely
To do offence ?

John. Yes, marry, and they urg'd it
As far as they had spirit.

Fred. Pray go forward.

John. A gentleman I found engag'd amongst 'em,
It seems of noble breeding, I'm sure brave metal ;

As I return'd to look you, I set into him,
And without hurt, I thank Heaven, rescu'd him.

　Fred. My work's done then :
And now to satisfy you there is a woman,
Oh, John! there is a woman—

　　John. Oh, where is she?

　　Fred. And one of no less worth than I told ;
And which is more, fall'n under my protection.

　　John. I am glad of that; forward, sweet Frederick.

　　Fred. And which is more than that, by this night's
　　　　wand'ring;
And which is most of all, she is at home too, sir.

　　John. Come, let's begone then.

　　Fred. Yes, but 'tis most certain,
You cannot see her, John.

　　John. Why?

　　Fred. She has sworn me,
That none else shall come near her ; not my mother,
Till some doubts are clear'd.

　　John. Not look upon her? What chamber is she in?

　　Fred. In ours.

　　John. Let's go, I say :
A woman's oaths are wafers and break with making.
They must for modesty a little : We all know it.

　　Fred. No, I'll assure ye, sir.

　　John. Not see her!
I smell an old dog-trick of yours. Well, Frederick,
Ye talk'd to me of whoring, let's have fair play,
Square dealing I would wish ye.

　　Fred. When 'tis come

(Which I know never will be) to that issue,
Your spoon shall be as deep as mine, sir.
    John. Tell me,
And tell me true, is the cause honourable,
Or for your ease?
    Fred. By all our friendship, John,
'Tis honest, and of great end.
    John. I'm answer'd;
But let me see her, tho': leave the door open
As you go in.
    Fred. I dare not.
    John. Not wide open,
But just so as a jealous husband
Would level at his wanton wife through.
    Fred. That courtesy,
If you desire no more, and keep it strictly,
I dare afford ye: come, 'tis now near morning.
                                        [*Exeunt.*

                Enter PETER *and* ANTHONY.

    Pet. Nay, the old woman's gone too.
    Ant. She's a cater-wauling
Amongst the gutters.   But conceive me, Peter,
Where our good masters should be,
    Pet. Where they should be,
I do conceive; but where they are, good Anthony—
    Ant. Ay, there it goes: my master's bo-peep with
        me,
With his sly popping in and out again,
Argu'd a cause—Hark!   [*Lute sounds.*

Pet. What?

Ant. Dost not hear a lute?

Again!

Pet. Where is't?

Ant. Above, in my master's chamber.

Pet. There's no creature : he hath the key himself,
Man.

Ant. This is his lute, let him have it.

[*Sings within a little.*

Pet. I grant ye ; but who strikes it?

Ant. An admirable voice too, hark ye.

Pet. Anthony,
Art sure we are at home?

Ant. Without all doubt, Peter.

Pet. Then this must be the devil.

Ant. Let it be;
Good devil, sing again : O dainty devil,
Peter, believe it, a most delicate devil,
The sweetest devil——

Enter FREDERICK *and Don* JOHN.

Fred. If you would leave peeping.

John. I cannot by no means.

Fred. Then come in softly ;
And as you love your faith, presume no further
Than ye have promis'd.

John. Basco.

Fred. What makes you up so early, sir?

John. You, sir, in your contemplations?

Pet. O pray ye peace, sir!

Fred. Why peace, sir?

Pet. Do you hear?

John. 'Tis your lute : she's playing on't.

Ant. The house is haunted, sir :

For this we have heard this half year.

Fred. Ye saw nothing?

Ant. Not I.

Pet. Nor I, sir.

Fred. Get your breakfast then,

And make no words on't : we'll undertake this spirit,

If it be one.

Ant. This is no devil, Peter:

Mum! there be bats abroad.   [*Exeunt ambo.*

Fred. Stay, now she sings.

John. An angel's voice, I'll swear,

Fred. Why dost thou shrug so?

Either allay this heat, or as I live,

I will not trust ye.

John. Pass, I warrant ye.   [*Exeunt.*

Enter 1st CONSTANTIA.

Con. To curse those stars that men say govern us,

To rail at fortune, to fall out with my fate,

And tax the general world, will help me nothing:

Alas! I am the same still, neither are they

Subject to helps or hurts ; our own desires

Are our own fates, and our own stars all our fortune ;

Which as we sway 'em, so abuse or bless us.

Enter FREDERICK *and Don* JOHN *peeping.*

Fred. Peace to your meditations.

John. Pox upon ye,
Stand out of the light.

Con. I crave your mercy, sir !
My mind, o'ercharg'd with care, made me unmannerly.

Fred. Pray ye set that mind at rest, all shall be perfect.

John. I like the body rare ; a handsome body,
A wond'rous handsome body ; would she would turn :
See, and that spightful puppy be not got
Between me and my light again.

Fred. 'Tis done,
As all that you command shall be :
The gentleman is safely off all danger.

John. Rare creature !

Con. How shall I thank ye, sir ? how satisfy ?

Fred. Speak softly, gentle lady, all's rewarded.
Now does he melt like marmalade.

John. Nay, 'tis certain,
Thou art the sweetest woman that eyes e'er look'd on.

Fred. Has none disturb'd ye ?

Con. Not any, sir, nor any sound came near me ;
I thank your care.

Fred. 'Tis well.

John. I would fain pray now,
But the devil, and that flesh there o'th' world——
What are we made to suffer ?

Fred. He'll enter—
Pull in your head and be hang'd.

John. Hark ye, Frederick,
I have brought you home your pack-saddle.

Fred. Pox upon ye.

Con. Nay, let him enter—Fie, my lord the duke,
Stand peeping at your friends.

Fred. Ye are cozen'd, lady,
Here is no duke.

Con. I know him full well, signior.

John. Hold thee there, wench.

Fred. This mad-brain'd fool will spoil all.

Con. I do beseech your grace come in.

John. My grace!
There was a word of comfort.

Fred. Shall he enter,
Whoe'er he be?

John. Well follow'd, Frederick.

Con. With all my heart.

Enter Don JOHN.

Fred. Come in then.

John. Bless ye, lady.

Fred. Nay, start not; tho' he be a stranger to ye,
He's of a noble strain, my kinsman, lady,
My countryman, and fellow-traveller;
One bed contains us ever, one purse feeds us,
And one faith free between us: do not fear him,
He's truly honest.

John. That's a lie.

Fred. And trusty,
Beyond your wishes: valiant to defend,
And modest to converse with, as your blushes.

John. Now may I hang myself; this commendation
Has broke the neck of all my hopes: for now
Must I cry, no forsooth, and ay forsooth, and surely,
And truly as I live, and as I am honest.
He's done these things for nonce too; for he knows,
Like a most envious rascal as he is,
I am not honest
This way: he'as watch'd his time,
But I shall quit him.

Con. Sir, I credit ye.

Fred. Go salute her, John.

John. Plague o' your commendations.

Con. Sir, I shall now desire to be a trouble.

John. Never to me, sweet lady; thus I seal
My faith, and all my services.

Con. One word, signior.

John. Now 'tis impossible I should be honest.
What points she at? My leg, I warrant; or
My well-knit body: sit fast, Don Frederick.

Fred. 'Twas given him by that gentleman
You took such care of; his own being lost i'th' scuffle.

Con. With much joy may he wear it; 'tis a right
      one,
I can assure ye, gentlemen, and right happy
May he be in all fights for that noble service.

Fred. Why do you blush?

Con. It had almost cozen'd me,

For, not to lie, when I saw that, I look'd for
Another owner of it : but 'tis well.

   Fred. Who's there ?   [*Knocks within.*
Stand ye a little close. Come in, sir.   [*Exit* Con.

Enter ANTHONY.

Now, what's the news with you ?

   Ant. There is a gentleman without
Would speak with Don John.

   John. Who, sir ?

   Ant. I do not know, sir, but he shews a man
Of no mean reckoning.

   Fred. Let him shew his name,
And then return a little wiser.   [*Exit* Ant.
How do you like her, John ?

   John. As well as you, Frederick,
For all I am honest ; you shall find it too.

   Fred. Art thou not honest ?

   John. Art thou an ass ?
And modest as her blushes ! What blockhead
Would e'er have popp'd out such a dry apology
For his dear friend ? and to a gentlewoman,
A woman of her youth and delicacy ?
They are arguments to draw them to abhor us.
An honest moral man ! 'tis for a constable ;
A handsome man, a wholesome man, a tough man,
A liberal man, a likely man, a man
Made up like Hercules, unslack'd with service ;
The same to-night, to-morrow night, the next night,
And so to perpetuity of pleasures :

These had been things to hearken to, things catching;
But you have such a spiced consideration,
Such qualms upon your worship's conscience,
Such chilblains in your blood, that all things prick ye,
Which nature and the liberal world make custom;
And nothing but fair honour, O sweet honour,
Hang up your eunuch honour.   That I was trusty,
And valiant, were things well put in; but modest!
A modest gentleman! O, wit, where was't thou?

 Fred. I am sorry, John.

 John. My lady's gentlewoman
Would laugh me to a school-boy, make me blush
With playing with my cod-piece point: fie on thee,
A man of thy discretion!

 Fred. It shall be mended;
And henceforth ye shall have your due.

Enter ANTHONY.

 John. I look for't.   How now, who is't?

 Ant. A gentleman of this city,
And calls himself Petruchio.

 John. I'll attend him.

Enter 1*st* CONSTANTIA.

 Con. How did he call himself?

 Fred. Petruchio.
Does it concern ye ought?

 Con. O, gentlemen,
The hour of my destruction is come on me,

E

I am discover'd, lost, left to my ruin—
As ever ye have pity——

John. Do not fear.
Let the great devil come, he shall come thro' me first:
Lost here, and we about ye!

Fred. Fall before us!

Con. O my unfortunate estate, all angers
Compar'd to his, to his——

Fred. Let his and all men's,
Whilst we have power and life, stand up for Heaven's
　　sake.

Con. I have offended Heaven too; yet Heaven
　　knows—

John. We are all evil:
Yet Heaven forbid we should have our deserts.
What is he?

Con. Too, too near my offence, sir:
O he will cut me piece-meal.

Fred. 'Tis no treason?

John. Let it be what it will? if he cut here,
I'll find him cut-work.

Fred. He must buy you dear,
With more than common lives.

John. Fear not, nor weep not:
By Heaven, I'll fire the town before ye perish,
And then the more the merrier, we'll jog with ye.

Fred. Come in, and dry your eyes.

John. Pray no more weeping:
Spoil a sweet face for nothing! My return

Shall end all this, I warrant ye.

Con. Heaven grant it may. [*Exeunt.*

Enter PETRUCHIO *with a letter.*

Petr. This man should be of quality and worth
By Don Alvaro's letter, for he gives
No slight recommendations of him :
I'll e'en make use of him.

Enter Don JOHN.

John. Save ye, sir. I am sorry
My business was so unmannerly, to make ye
Wait thus long here.

Petr. Occasions must be serv'd, sir :
But is your name Don John ?

John. It is, sir.

Petr. Then,
First for your own brave sake I must embrace ye :
Next, for the credit of your noble friend,
Hernanda de Alvara, make ye mine :
Who lays his charge upon me in this letter
To look ye out, and
Whilst your occasions make you resident
In this place, to supply ye, love and honour ye ;
Which had I known sooner————

John. Noble sir,
You'll make my thanks too poor : I wear a sword, sir,
And have a service to be still dispos'd of,
As you shall please command it.

Petr. That manly courtesy is half my business, sir :

E ij

And to be short, to make ye know I honour ye,
And in all points believe your worth like oracle,
This day, Petruchio,
A man that may command the strength of this place,
Hazard the boldest spirits, hath made choice
Only of you, and in a noble office.

   John. Forward, I am free to entertain it.

   Petr. Thus then,
I do beseech ye mark me.

   John. I shall, sir.

   Petr. Ferrara's Duke, would I might call him
      worthy,
But that he has raz'd out from his family,
As he has mine with infamy; this man,
Rather this powerful monster, we being left
But two of all our house to stock our memories,
My sister Constantia and myself, with arts and witch-
      crafts,
Vows and such oaths Heaven has no mercy for,
Drew to dishonour this weak maid by stealth,
And secret passages I knew not of.
Oft he obtain'd his wishes, oft abus'd her,
I am asham'd to say the rest: this purchas'd,
And his hot blood allay'd, he left her,
And all our name to ruin.

   John. This was foul play,
And ought to be rewarded so.

   Petr. I hope so.
He scap'd me yester-night;
Which if he dare again adventure for——

John. Pray, sir, what commands have you to lay
　　on me ?

Petr. Only thus; by word of mouth to carry him
A challenge from me, that so (if he have honour in
　　him)
We may decide all difference between us.

John. Fair and noble,
And I will do it home.　When shall I visit ye ?

Petr. Please you this afternoon, I will ride with you,
For at the castle six miles hence, we are sure
To find him.

John. I'll be ready.

Petr. My man shall wait here,
To conduct you to my house.

John. I shall not fail ye.　　　　　　　[*Exit* Petr.

Enter FREDERICK.

Fred. How now ?

John. All's well, and better than thou couldst expect, for this wench here is certainly no maid : and I
have hopes she is the same that our two curious cox-
combs have been so long a hunting after.

Fred. Why do ye hope so ?

John. Why, because first she is no maid, and next
because she is handsome ; there are two reasons for
you : now do you find out a third, a better if you
can.　For take this Frederick for a certain rule, since
she loves the sport, she'll never give it over; and
therefore (if we have good luck) in time may fall to
our share.

Fred. Very pretty reasons indeed! But I thought you had known some particular, that made you conclude this to be the woman.

John. Yes, I know her name is Constantia.

Fred. That now is something; but I cannot believe her dishonest for all this: she has not one loose thought about her.

John. It's no matter, she's loose i' th' hilts, by Heaven. There has been stirring, fumbling with linen, Frederick.

Fred. There may be such a slip.

John. And will be, Frederick, whilst the old game's a-foot. I fear the boy too will prove her's I took up.

Fred. Good circumstances may cure all this yet.

John. There thou hit'st it, Frederick. Come, let's walk in, and comfort her—that she is here, is nothing yet suspected. Anon I shall tell thee why her brother came, (who by this light is a noble fellow) and what honour he has done to me, a stranger, in calling me to serve him. There be irons heating for some, on my word, Frederick.   [*Exeunt.*

ACT III. SCENE I.

Enter Landlady and ANTHONY.

Landlady.

COME, sir, who is it keeps your master company?

Ant. I say to you, Don John.

Land. I say what woman?

Ant. I say so too.

Land. I say again, I will know.

Ant. I say 'tis fit you should.

Land. And I tell thee he has a woman here.

Ant. I tell thee 'tis then the better for him.

Land. Was ever gentlewoman
So frumpt up with a fool? Well, saucy, sirrah,
I will know who it is, and to what purpose.
I pay the rent, and I will know how my house
Comes by these inflammations. If this geer hold,
Best hang a sign-post up, to tell the signiors,
Here you may have lewdness at livery.

Enter FREDERICK.

Ant. 'Twould be a great ease to your age.

Fred. How now?
What's the matter, Landlady?

Land. What's the matter!
Ye use me decently among ye, gentlemen.

Fred. Who has abus'd her? You, sir?

Land. Od's my witness,
I will not be thus treated, that I will not.

Ant. I gave her no ill language.

Land. Thou liest lewdly;
Thou took'st me up at every word I spoke,
As I had been a maukin, a flirt gillian:
And thou think'st, because thou canst write and read,
Our noses must be under thee.

Fred. Dare you so, sirrah?

Ant. Let but the truth be known, sir, I beseech ye—
She raves of wenches, and I know not what, sir.

Land. Go to, thou know'st too well, thou wicked
varlet,
Thou instrument of evil.

Ant. As I live, sir, she's ever thus till dinner.

Fred. Get ye in, I'll answer ye anon, sir. [*Exit* Ant.
Now your grief, what is't? for I can guess——

Land. Ye may, with shame enough,
If there were shame amongst you—nothing thought on,
But how ye may abuse my house : not satisfy'd
With bringing home your bastards to undo me,
But you must drill your whores here too ; my patience,
Because I bear, and bear, and carry all,
And as they say, am willing to groan under,
Must be your make-sport now.

Fred. No more of these words,
Nor no more murmurings, lady : for you know
That I know something. I did suspect your anger,
But turn it presently and handsomely,
And bear yourself discreetly to this woman,
For such a one there is indeed.

Land. 'Tis well, sir.

Fred. Leave off your devil's matins, and your me-
lancholies,
Or we shall leave our lodgings.

Land. You have much need
To use the vagrant ways, and too much profit :
Ye had that might content,

(At home within yourselves too) right good, gen-
     tlemen,
Wholesome, and ye said handsome. But you, gallants,
Beast that I was to believe ye——

    Fred. Leave your suspicion;
For as I live there's no such thing.

    Land. Mine honour;
And 'twere not for mine honour——

    Fred. Come, your honour,
Your house, and you too, if you dare believe me
Are well enough: sleek up yourself, leave crying,
For I must have ye entertain this lady
With all civility, she well deserves it,
Together with all service: I dare trust ye,
For I have found ye faithful. When you know her,
You will find your own fault; no more words, but
    do it.

    Land. You know you may command me.

        Enter Don JOHN.

    John. Worshipful lady,
How does thy velvet scabbard? By this hand ·
Thou look'st most amiably. Now could I willingly
(And 'twere not for abusing thy Geneva print there)
Venture my body with thee——

    Land. You'll leave this roguery
When ye come to my years.

    John. By this light,
Thou art not above fifteen yet; a mere girl,
Thou hast not half thy teeth——

Fred. Pr'ythee, John,
Let her alone, she has been vex'd already:
She'll grow stark mad, man,
    John. I would fain see her mad.
An old mad woman—
    Fred. Pr'ythee, be patient.
    John. Is like a miller's mare, troubled with tooth-
       ache;
She makes the rarest faces——
    Fred. Go, and do it,
And do not mind this fellow.
       [*Exit Landlady, and comes back again presently.*
    John. What, agen!
Nay, then it is decreed; tho' hills were set on hills,
And seas met seas, to guard thee, I would through.
    Land. Odd's my witness, if you ruffle me, I'll spoil
your sweet face for you, that I will. Go, go to the
door, there's a gentleman there would speak with ye.
    John. Upon my life, Petruchio. Good, dear Land-
lady, carry him into the dining-room, and I'll wait
upon him presently.
    Land. Well, Don John, the time will come that I
shall be even with you.   [*Exit.*
    John. I must be gone; yet if my project hold,
You shall not stay behind: I'll rather trust
A cat with sweet milk, Frederick. By her face,

       Enter 1st CONSTANTIA.

I feel her fears are working.
    Con. Is there no way,

I do beseech ye, think yet, to divert
This certain danger?

Fred. 'Tis impossible:
Their honours are engag'd.

Con. Then there must be murder,
Which, gentlemen, I shall no sooner hear of,
Than make one in't. You may, if you please, sir,
Make all go less.

John. Lady, were't my own cause,
I could dispense; but loaden with my friend's trust,
I must go on, tho' general massacres
As much I fear——

Con. Do you hear, Sir? for Heaven's sake,
Let me request one favour of you.

Fred. Yes, any thing.

Con. This gentleman I find is too resolute,
Too hot and fiery for the cause: as ever
You did a virtuous deed, for honour's sake,
Go with him, and allay him: your fair temper,
A noble disposition, like wish'd showers,
May quench those eating fires, that would spoil all else.
I see in him destruction.

Fred. I will do it:
And 'tis a wise consideration,
To me a bounteous favour. Hark ye, John,
I will go with ye.

John. No.

Fred. Indeed I will——
Ye go upon a hazard—no denial—
For as I live I'll go.

John. Then make ye ready,
For I am straight on horseback.

Fred. My sword on, and
I am as ready as you. What my best labour,
With all the art I have can work upon 'em,
Be sure of, and expect a fair end : the old gentlewoman
Shall wait upon ye; she is discreet and secret,
Ye may trust her in all points.

Con. Ye are noble ;
And so I take my leave.

John. I hope, lady, a happy issue for all this.

Con. All heaven's care upon ye, and my prayers.

John. So,
Now my mind's at rest.

Fred. Away, 'tis late, John.   [*Exeunt.*

     Enter ANTONIO, *Surgeon and a Gentleman.*

Gent. What symptoms do ye find in him ?

Sur. None, sir, dangerous, if he'd be ruled.

Gent. Why, what does he do ?

Sur. Nothing that he should. First, he will let
no liquor down but wine, and then he has a fancy
that he must be dressed always to the tune of John
Dory.

Gent. How, to the tune of John Dory ?

Sur. Why, he will have fidlers, and make them
play and sing it to him all the while.

Gent. An odd fancy indeed.

Ant. Give me some wine.

Sur. I told ye so——'Tis death, sir.

Ant. 'Tis a horse, sir. Dost thou think I shall recover with the help of barley-water only?

Gent. Fie, Antonio, you must be governed.

Ant. Why sir, he feeds me with nothing but rotten roots and drowned chickens, stewed *pericraniums* and *pia-maters*; and when I go to bed (by Heaven 'tis true, sir) he rolls me up in lints, with labels at 'em, that I am just the man i'th' almanack, my head and face is in Aries' place.

Sur. Will it please ye, to let your friends see you opened.

Ant. Will it please you, sir, to give me a brimmer? I feel my body open enough for that. Give it me, or I'll die upon thy hand, and spoil thy custom.

Sur. How, a brimmer?

Ant. Why look ye, sir, thus I am used still; I can get nothing that I want. In how long time canst thou cure me?

Sur. In forty days.

Ant. I'll have a dog shall lick me whole in twenty. In how long canst thou kill me?

Sur. Presently.

Ant. Do it: that's the shorter, and there's more delight in it.

Gent. You must have patience.

Ant. Man, I must have business—this foolish fellow hinders himself—I have a dozen rascals to hurt within these five days. Good man-mender, stop me up with parsley, like stuffed beef, and let me walk abroad.

Sur. You shall walk shortly.

Ant. I will walk presently, sir, and leave your sal-
lads there, your green salves, and your oils; I'll to
my old diet again, strong food, and rich wine, and
try what that will do.

Sur. Well, go thy ways, thou art the maddest old
fellow I ever met with.   [*Exeunt.*

Enter 1st CONSTANTIA *and Landlady.*

Con. I have told ye all I can, and more than yet
Those gentlemen know of me.   But are they
such strange creatures, say you?

Land. There's the younger,
Don John, the errant'st Jack in all this city:
The other time has blasted, yet he will stoop,
If not o'er-flown, and freely, on the quarry—
Has been a dragon in his days.   But, Tarmont,
Don Jenken, is the devil himself—the dog-days—
The most incomprehensible whore-master——
Twenty a night is nothing : the truth is,
Whose chastity he chops upon he cares not,
He flies at all—bastards, upon my conscience,
He has now in making multitudes—The last night
He brought home one ; I pity her that bore it,
But we are all weak vessels.   Some rich woman
(For wise I dare not call her) was the mother,
For it was hung with jewels ; the bearing cloth
No less than crimson velvet.

Con. How!

Land. 'Tis true, lady.

Con. Was it a boy too?

Land. A brave boy; deliberation,
And judgment shew'd in's getting, as I'll say for him.
He's as well plac'd for that sport——

Con. May I see it?
For there is a neighbour of mine, a gentlewoman,
Has had a late mischance, which willingly
I would know further of; now if you please
To be so courteous to me.

Land. Ye shall see it.
But what do you think of these men, now ye know
        'em?
Be wise,
Ye may repent too late else; I but tell ye
For your own good, and as you will find it, lady.

Con. I am advis'd.

Land. No more words then; do that,
And instantly, I told ye of: be ready.
Don John, I'll fit ye for your frumps.

Con. " It shall be."
But shall I see this child?

Land. Within this half hour.
Let's in, and think better.   [*Exeunt.*

Enter PETRUCHIO, *Don* JOHN, *and* FREDERICK.

John. Sir, he is worth your knowledge, and a
        gentleman
(If I that so much love him may commend him)
That's full of honour; and one, if foul play

F ij

Should fall upon us, (for which fear I brought him)
Will not fly back for filips.

Petr. Ye much honour me,
And once more I pronounce ye both mine.

Fred. Stay, what troop
Is that below i' th' valley there?

John. Hawking, I take it.

Petr. They are so; 'tis the duke, 'tis even he,
gentlemen.
Sirrah, draw back the horses till we call ye.
I know him by his company.

Fred. I think too,
He bends up this way.

Petr. So he does.

John. Stand you still,
Within that covert, till I call. He comes forward;
Here will I wait him. To your places.

Petr. I need no more instruct ye.

John. Fear me not.   [*Exeunt* Petr. *and* Fred.

Enter DUKE *and his faĉtion.*

Duke. Feed the hawks up,
We'll fly no more to-day. O my blest fortune,
Have I so fairly met the man?

John. Ye have, sir,
And him ye know by this.

Duke. Sir, all the honour,
And love——

John. I do beseech your grace stay there.
Dismiss your train a little.

Duke. Walk aside,
And out of hearing, I command ye.
Now, sir, be plain.

John. I will, and short.
Ye have wrong'd a gentleman beyond all justice,
Beyond the mediation of all friends.

Duke. The man, and manner of wrong?

John. Petruchio;
The wrong, ye have dishonoured his sister.

Duke. Now stay you, sir,
And hear me a little. This gentleman's
Sister that you nam'd, 'tis true I have long lov'd;
As true I have enjoy'd her : no less truth,
I have a child by her. But that she, or he,
Or any of that family are tainted,
Suffer disgrace, or ruin, by my pleasures;
I wear a sword to satisfy the world no,
And him in this cause when he pleases; for know, sir,
She is my wife, contracted before Heaven;
(A witness I owe more tie to than her brother)
Nor will I fly from that name, which long since
Had had the church's approbation,
But for his jealous nature.

John. Your pardon, sir, I am fully satisfied.

Duke. Dear sir, I knew I should convert ye.
Had we but that rough man here now to——

John. And ye shall, sir.
What, hoa, hoa!

Duke. I hope you have laid no ambush?

Enter PETRUCHIO.

John. Only friends.

Duke. My noble brother, welcome.
Come, put your anger off, we'll have no fighting,
Unless you will maintain I am unworthy
To bear that name.

Petr. Do you speak this heartily?

Duke. Upon my soul, and truly; the first priest
Shall put ye out of these doubts.

Petr. Now I love ye,
And I beseech ye, pardon my suspicions;
You are now more than a brother, a brave friend too.

John. The good man's over-joy'd.

Enter FREDERICK.

Fred. How now goes it?

John. Why the man has his mare again, and all's
     well.
The duke professes freely he's her husband.

Fred. 'Tis a good hearing.

John. Yes, for modest gentlemen. I must present ye.
May it please your grace,
To number this brave gentleman, my friend,
And noble kinsman, among the rest of your servants.

Duke. O my brave friend, you shower your boun-
     ties on me.
Amongst my best thoughts, signior, in which number
You being worthily dispos'd already,
May freely place your friend.

Fred. Your grace does me a great deal of honour.

Petr. Why this is wond'rous happy. But now, brother,

Now comes the bitter to our sweet——Constantia——

Duke. Why, what of her?

Petr. Nor what, nor where do I know.

Wing'd with her fears, last night, beyond my knowledge,

She quit my house, but whether——

Fred. Let not that——

Duke. No more, good sir, I have heard too much.

Petr. Nay, sink not,

She cannot be so lost.

John. Nor shall not, gentlemen :

Be free again, the lady's found.   That smile, sir,

Shews you distrust your servant.

Duke. I do beseech ye——

John. Ye shall believe me ; by my soul she's safe.

Duke. Heaven knows I would believe, sir.

Fred. Ye may safely.

John. And under noble usage. This gentleman

Met her in all her doubts last night, and to his guard

(Her fears being strong upon her) she gave her person,

Who waited on her to our lodging ; where all respect,

Civil and honest service, now attend her.

Petr. Ye may believe now.

Duke. Yes, I do, and strongly.

Well, my good friends, or rather my good angels,

For ye have both preserv'd me ; when these virtues
Die in your friend's remembrance———

John. Good your grace,
Lose no more time in compliments, 'tis too precious ;
I know it by myself, there can be no hell
To his that hangs upon his hopes.

Petr. He has hit it.

Fred. To horse again then, for this night I'll crown
With all the joys ye wish for.

Petr. Happy gentlemen.   [*Exeunt.*

Enter FRANCISCO *and a Man.*

Fran. This is the maddest mischief—never fool was
so fobb'd off as I am—made ridiculous, and to myself, to my own ass———trust a woman! I'll trust the
devil first, for he dares me better than his word sometimes. Pray tell me, in what observance have I ever
fail'd her ?

Man. Nay, you can tell that best yourself.

Fran. Let me consider———

Enter Don FREDERICK *and* JOHN.

Fred. Let them talk, we'll go on before.

Fran. Where didst thou meet Constantia and this
woman?

Fred. Constantia! What are these fellows ? Stay
by all means.

Man. Why, sir, I met her in the great street that

comes from the market-place, just at the turning, by a goldsmith's shop.

Fred. Stand still, John.

Fran. Well, Constantia has spun herself a fair thread now: what will her best friends think of this?

Fred. John, I smell some juggling, John.

John. Yes, Frederick, I fear it will be proved so.

Fran. But what should the reason be, dost think, of this so sudden change in her?

Fred. 'Tis she.

Man. Why, truly I suspect she has been entic'd to it by a stranger.

John. Did you mark that, Frederick?

Fran. Stranger! who?

Man. A young gentleman that's newly come to town.

Fred. Mark that too.

John. Yes, sir.

Fran. Why do ye think so?

Man. I heard her grave conductress twattle something as they went along, that makes me guess it.

John. 'Tis she, Frederick.

Fred. But who that he is, John?

Fran. I do not doubt to bolt them out, for they must certainly be about the town. Ha! no more words. Come, let's be gone. [*Exeunt* Francisco *and Man.*

Fred. Well.

John. Very well.

Fred. Discreetly.

John. Finely carried.

Fred. Ye have no more of these tricks;

John. Ten to one, sir, I shall meet with them if ye have.

Fred. Is this fair?

John. Was it in you a friend's part to deal double? I am no ass, Don Frederick.

Fred. And, Don John, it shall appear I am no fool: disgrace me to make yourself thus every woman's courtesy; 'tis boyish, 'tis base.

John. 'Tis false; I privy to this dog-trick! Clear yourself, for I know well enough where the wind sits; or as I have a life—   [*Trampling within.*

Fred. No more; they are coming; shew no discontent, let's quietly away. If she be at home, our jealousies are over; if not, you and I must have a farther parley, John.

John. Yes, Don Frederick, ye may be sure we shall. But where are these fellows? Pox on't, we have lost them too in our spleens, like fools.

Enter DUKE *and* PETRUCHIO.

Duke. Come, gentlemen, let's go a little faster;
Suppose you have all mistresses, and mend
Your pace accordingly.

John. Sir, I should be as glad of a mistress as another man.

Fred. Yes, o' my conscience wouldst thou, and of any other man's mistress too, that I'll answer for.

                                    [*Exeunt.*

Enter ANTONIO *and his Man.*

Ant. With all my gold?

Man. The trunk broken open, and all gone.

Ant. And the mother in the plot?

Man. And the mother and all.

Ant. And the devil and all; the mighty pox go with them. Belike they thought I was no more of this world, and those trifles would but disturb my conscience.

Man. Sure they thought, sir, you would not live to disturb them.

Ant. Well, my sweet mistrest, I'll try how handsomely your ladyship can hang upon a pair of gallows; there's your master-piece. No imagination where they should be?

Man. None, sir; yet we have searched all places we suspected; I believe they have taken towards the port.

Ant. Get me then a water-conjuror, one that can raise water-devils. I'll port them! play at duck and drake with my money! Get me a conjuror, I say; inquire out a man that lets out devils.

Man. I don't know where.

Ant. In every street, Tom Fool; any blear-ey'd people with red heads and flat noses can perform it. Thou shalt know them by their half gowns, and no breeches. Find me out a conjuror, I say, and learn his price, how he will let his devils out by the day. I'll have them again if they be above ground.

[*Exeunt.*

1

Enter DUKE, PETRUCHIO, FREDERICK, *and Don*
JOHN.

Petr. Your grace is welcome now to Naples, so ye
are all, gentlemen.

John. Don Frederick, will you step in, and give the
lady notice who comes to visit her?

Petr. Bid her make haste; we come to see no curious wench, a night-gown will serve our turn. Here's
one that knows her nearer.

Fred. I'll tell her what you say, sir.   [*Exit.*

Petr. Now will the sport be, to observe her altera-
tions, how betwixt fear and joy she will behave herself.

Duke. Dear brother, I must intreat you————

Petr. I conceive your mind, sir—I will not chide
her.

Enter FREDERICK *and* PETER.

John. How now?

Fred. You may, sir; not to abuse your patience,
longer, nor hold ye off with tedious circumstances;
for ye must know————

Petr. What?

Duke. Where is she?

Fred. Gone, sir.

Duke. How!

Petr. What did you say, sir?

Fred. Gone; by Heaven removed. The woman of
the house too.

2

Petr. What, that reverend old woman that tired me with compliments ?

Fred. The very same.

John. Well, Don Frederick.

Fred. Don John, it is not well—But———

Petr. Gone!

Fred. This fellow can satisfy I lie not.

Pet. A little after my master was departed, sir, with this gentleman, my fellow and myself being sent on business, as we must think on purpose———

Petr. Hang these circumstances, they always serve to usher in ill ends.

John. Now could I eat that rogue, I am so angry. Gone!

Petr. Gone!

Fred. Directly gone, fled, shifted; what would you have me say ?

Duke. Well, gentlemen, wrong not my good opinion.

Fred. For your dukedom, sir, I would not be a knave.

John. He that is, a rot run in his blood.

Petr. But, hark ye, gentlemen, are you sure you had her here? Did you not dream this ?

John. Have you your nose, sir ?

Petr. Yes, sir.

John. Then we had her.

Petr. Since ye are so short, believe your having her shall suffer more construction.

John. Well, sir, let it suffer.

Fred. How to convince ye, sir, I can't imagine; but my life shall justify my innocence, or fall with it.

Duke. Thus then——for we may be all abused.

Petr. 'Tis possible.

Duke. Here let's part until to-morrow this time; we to our way to clear this doubt, and you to yours: pawning our honours then to meet again; when if she be not found—

Fred. We stand engag'd to answer any worthy way we are call'd to.

Duke. We ask no more.

Petr. To-morrow certain.

John. If we out-live this night, sir.

[*Exeunt* Duke *and* Petruchio.

Fred. Come, Don John, we have somewhat now to do.

John. I am sure I would have.

Fred. If she be not found, we must fight.

John. I am glad on't, I have not fought a great while.

Fred. If we die—

John. There's so much money saved in letchery.

[*Exeunt.*

ACT IV. SCENE I.

Enter 2d CONSTANTIA, *and her Mother.*

Mother.

HOLD, Cons, hold, for goodness hold, I am in that desertion of spirit for want of breath, that I am almost reduced to the necessity of not being able to defend myself against the inconvenience of a fall.

2d Con. Dear mother, let us go a little faster to secure ourselves from Antonio: for my part I am in that terrible fright, that I can neither think, speak, nor stand still, till we are safe a ship-board, and out of sight of the shore.

Moth. Out of sight o'the shore! why, d'ye think I'll depatriate?

2d Con. Depratiate! what's that?

Moth. Why, ye fool you, leave my country: what will you never learn to speak out of the vulgar road?

2d Con. O Lord, this hard word will undo us.

Moth. As I am a Christian, if it were to save my honour (which is ten thousand times dearer to me than my life) I would not be guilty of so odious a thought.

2d Con. Pray, mother, since your honour is so dear to ye, consider that if we are taken, both it and we are lost for ever.

Moth. Ay, Girl; but what will the world say, if they should hear so odious a thing of us, as that we should depatriate?

2d Con. Ay, there's it; the world! why, mother, the world does not care a pin, if both you and I were hang'd; and that we shall be certainly, if Antonio takes us, for running away with his gold.

Moth. Protest I care not, I'll ne'er depart from the demarches of a person of quality; and let come what will, I shall rather choose to submit myself to my

G ij

fate, than strive to prevent by any deportment that is not congruous in every degree, to the steps and measures of a strict practitioner of honour.

2d Con. Would not this make one stark mad? Her style is not more out of the way, than her manner of reasoning: she first sells me to an ugly old fellow, then she runs away with me and all his gold, and now, like a strict practitioner of honour, resolves to be taken, rather than depratiate, as she calls it. [*Aside.*

Moth. As I am a Christian, Cons, here's a tavern, and a very decent sign : I'll in, I am resolv'd, tho' by it I should run a risco of never so supendous a nature.

2d Con. There's no stopping her. What shall I do?

Moth. I'll send for my kinswoman and some music to revive me a little : for really, Cons, I am reduced to that sad imbecility by the injury I have done my poor feet, that I'm in a great incertitude, whether they will have liveliness sufficient to support me up to the top of the stairs, or no.   [*Exit.*

2d Con. This sinning without pleasure, I cannot endure : to have always remorse, and ne'er do any thing that should cause it, is intolerable. If I lov'd money too, which I think I don't, my mother she has all that : I have nothing to comfort myself with, but Antonio's stiff beard ; and that alone, for a woman of my years, is but a sorry kind of entertainment. I wonder why these old fumbling fellows should trouble themselves so much, only to trouble us more. They can do nothing, but put us in mind of our graves,

Well, I'll no more on't; for to be frighted with death and damnation both at once, is a little too hard. I do here vow I'll live for ever chaste, or find out some handsome young fellow I can love; I think that's the better.   [*Mother looks out at the window.*

Moth. Come up, Cons, the fiddles are here.

2d Con. I come——   [*Mother goes from the window.* I must be gone, tho' whither I cannot tell. These fiddles, and her discreet companions, will quickly make an end of all she has stolen; and then five hundred new pieces sell me to another old fellow. She has taken care not to leave me a farthing: yet I am so, better than under her conduct: 'twill be at worst but begging for my life.

And starving were to me an easier fate,
Than to be forc'd to live with one I hate.
                    [*Goes up to her Mother.*

Enter Don JOHN.

John. It will not out of my head, but that Don Frederick has sent away this wench, for all he carries it so gravely; yet methinks he should be honester than so: but these grave men are never touch'd upon such occasions. Mark it when you will, and you'll find a grave man, especially if he pretend to be a precise man, will do ye forty things without remorse, that would startle one of us mad fellows to think of. Because they are familiar with Heaven in their prayers, they think they may be bold with it in any thing;

now we that are not so well acquainted, bear greater reverence.   [*Music plays above.*

What's here, music and women? Wou'd I had one of 'em.   [*One of 'em looks out at the window.*

That's a whore; I know it by her smile. O' my conscience, take a woman masked and hooded, nay cover'd all o'er, so that you cannot see one bit of her, and at twelvescore yards distance, if she be a whore, as ten to one she is, I shall know it certainly; I have an instinct within me ne'er fails.   [*Another looks out.* Ah, rogue! she's right too I'm sure on't.

Moth. above. Come, come, let's dance in t'other room, 'tis a great deal better.

John. Say you so; what now if I should go up and dance too? It is a tavern; pox o'this business: I'll in, I am resolv'd, and try my own fortune; 'tis hard luck if I don't get one of 'em.

As he goes to the door, 2d CONSTANTIA *enters.*

See here's one bolted already; fair lady, whither so fast?

2d Con. I don't know, sir.

John. May I have the honour to wait upon you?

2d Con. Yes, if you please, sir.

John. Whither;

2d Con. I tell you, I don't know.

John. She's very quick. Would I might be so happy as to know you, lady.

2d Con. I dare not let you see my face, sir.

John. Why?

2d Con. For fear you should not like it, and then leave me; for to tell ye true, I have at this present very great need of you.

John. If thou hast half so much need of me, as I have of thee, lady, I'll be content to be hanged tho'.

2d Con. It's a proper handsome fellow this, if he'd but love me now, I would never seek out further. Sir, I am young, and unexperienced in the world.

John. Nay, if thou art young, it's no great matter what thy face is.

2d Con. Perhaps this freedom in me may seem strange; but, sir, in short, I'm forced to fly from one I hate; if I should meet him, will you here promise he shall not take me from you.

John. Yes, that I will before I see your face, your shape has charmed me enough for that already; if any one takes ye from me, lady, I'll give him leave to take from me two—(I was going to name 'em) certain things of mine, that I would not lose, now I have you in my power, for all the gems in Christendom.

2d Con. For heaven's sake then conduct me to some place, where I may be secured awhile from the sight of any one whatsoever.

John. By all the hopes I have to find thy face as lovely as thy shape, I will.

2d Con. Well, sir, I believe ye; for you have an honest look.

John. 'Slid! I am afraid Don Frederick has been

giving her a character of me too. Come, pray un-mask.

2d Con. Then turn away your face; for I'm re-solved you shall not see a bit of mine till I have set it in order; and then——

John. What?

2d Con. I'll strike you dead.

John. A mettled whore, I warrant her: come, if she be now young, and have but a nose on her face, she'll be as good as her word. I'm e'en panting for breath already.

2d Con. Now stand your ground, if you dare.

John. By this light a rare creature! ten thousand times handsomer than her we seek for! This can be sure no common one: pray Heaven she be a whore.

2d Con. Well, sir, what say you now?

John. Nothing; I'm so amazed I am not able to speak. I'd best fall too presently, tho' it be in the street, for fear of losing time. Pr'ythee, my dear sweet creature, go with me into that corner, that thou and I may talk a little in private.

2d Con. No, sir, no private dealing, I beseech you.

John. 'Sheart, what shall I do? I'm out of my wits for her. Hark ye, my dear soul, canst thou love me?

2d Con. If I could, what then?

John. Why you know what then, and then should I be the happiest man alive.

2d Con. Ay, so you all say, till you have your de-sires, and then you leave us.

John. But, my dear heart, I am not made like other men : I never can love heartily till I have——

2d Con. Got their maidenheads ; but suppose now I should be no maid.

John. Pr'ythee suppose me nothing, but let me try.

2d Con. Nay, good sir, hold.

John. No maid ! Why, so much the better, thou art then the more experienced ; for my part, I hate a bungler at any thing.

2d Con. O dear, I like this fellow strangely. Hark ye, sir, I am not worth a groat, but tho' you should not be so neither, if you'll but love me, I'll follow ye all the world over : I'll work for ye, beg for ye, do any thing for ye, so you'll promise to do nothing with any body else.

John. O heavens, I'm in another world, this wench sure was made on purpose for me, she is so just of my humour. My dear, 'tis impossible for me to say how much I will do for thee, or with thee, thou sweet bewitching woman ; but let's make haste home, or I shall ne'er be able to hold out till I come thither.

[*Exeunt.*

Enter FREDERICK *and* FRANCISCO.

Fred. And art thou sure it was Constantia, say'st thou, that he was leading ?

Fran. Am I sure I live, sir ? Why, I dwelt in the house with her ; how can I choose but know her ?

Fred. But didst thou see her face ?

Fran. Lord, sir, I saw her face as plainly as I see yours just now, not two streets off.

Fred. Yes, 'tis even so : I suspected it at first, but then he forswore it with that confidence—Well, Don John, if these be your practices, you shall have no more a friend of me, sir, I assure you. Perhaps tho' he met her by chance, and intends to carry her to her brother, and the Duke.

Enter Don JOHN *and* 2d CONSTANTIA.

A little time will shew—God-so, here he is;
I'll step behind this shop, and observe what he says.

John. Here now go in, and make me for ever happy.

Fred. Dear Don John.

John. A pox o' your kindness. How the devil comes he here just at this time ? Now will he ask me forty foolish questions, and I have such a mind to this wench, that I cannot think of one excuse for my life.

Fred. Your servant, sir : pray who's that you locked in just now at the door ?

John. Why a friend of mine that's gone up to read a book.

Fred. A book ! that's a quaint one, i'faith : pr'ythee, Don John, what library hast thou been buying this afternoon ? for i' the morning, to my knowledge, thou hadst never a book there, except it were an almanack, and that was none of thy own neither.

John. No, no, it's a book of his own, he brought along with him : a scholar that's given to reading.

Fred. And do scholars, Don John, wear petticoats now-a-days ?

John. Plague on him, he has seen her—Well, Don Frederick, thou know'st I am not good at lying; 'tis a woman, I confess it, make your best on't : what then ?

Fred. Why then, Don John, I desire you'll be pleased to let me see her.

John. Why faith, Frederick, I should not be against the thing, but ye know a man must keep his word, and she has a mind to be private.

Fred. But, John, you may remember when I met a lady so before, this very self-same lady too, that I got leave for you to see her, John.

John. Why, do you think then that this here is Constantia ?

Fred. I cannot properly say I think it, John, because I know it; this fellow here saw her as you led her i' th' streets.

John. Well, and what then ? Who does he say it is ?

Fred. Ask him, sir, and he'll tell ye.

John. Sweet-heart, dost thou know this lady ?

Fran I think I should, sir; I have lived long enough in the house to know her sure.

John. And how do they call her, pr'ythee ?

Fran. Constantia.

John. How! Constantia.

Fran. Yes, sir, the woman's name is Constantia, that's flat.

John. Is it so, sir? and so is this too.   [*Strikes him.*

Fran. Oh, Oh!   [*Runs out.*

John. Now, sirrah, you may safely say you have not borne false witness for nothing.

Fred. Fie, Don John, why do you beat the poor fellow for doing his duty, and telling truth?

John. Telling truth! thou talk'st as if thou hadst been hir'd to bear false witness too: you are a very fine gentleman.

Fred. What a strange confidence he has! but is there no shame in thee? nor any consideration of what is just or honest, to keep a woman thus against her will, that thou knowest is in love with another man too? Dost think a judgment will not follow this?

John. Good, dear Frederick, do thou keep thy sentences and thy morals for some better opportunity; this here is not a fit subject for them: I tell thee, she is no more Constantia than thou art.

Fred. Why won't you let me see her then?

John. Because I can't: besides, she's not for thy turn.

Fred. How so?

John. Why, thy genius lies another way; thou art for flames and darts, and those fine things: now I am for the old, plain, downright way; I am not so curious, Frederick, as thou art.

Fred. Very well, sir; but is this worthy in you, to endeavour to debauch——

John. But is there no shame? but is this worthy? What a many buts are here? If I should tell thee now solemnly thou hast but one eye, and give thee reasons for it, wouldst thou believe me?

Fred. I think hardly, sir, against my own knowledge.

John. Then why dost thou, with that grave face, go about to persuade me against mine? You should do as you would be done by, Frederick.

Fred. And so I will, sir, in this very particular, since there's no other remedy; I shall do that for the Duke and Petruchio, which I should expect from them upon the like occasion: in short, to let you see I am as sensible of my honour, as you can be careless of yours; I must tell ye, sir, that I'm resolved to wait upon this lady to them.

John. Are ye so, sir? Why, I must then, sweet sir, tell you again, I am resolved you sha'nt. Ne'er stare nor wonder, I have promised to preserve her from the sight of any one whatsoever, and with the hazard of my life will make it good: but that you may not think I mean an injury to Petruchio, or the Duke, know, Don Frederick, that tho' I love a wench perhaps a little better, I hate to do a thing that's base as much as you do. Once more upon my honour, this is not Constantia; let that satisfy you.

Fred. All that will not do—— [*Goes to the door.*

John. No! why then this shall. [*Draws.*] Come not one step nearer, for if thou dost, by Heaven, it is thy last.

Fred. This is an insolence beyond the temper of a man to suffer——Thus I throw off thy friendship, and since thy folly has provoked my patience beyond its natural bounds, know it is not in thy power now to save thyself.

John. That's to be tried, sir, tho' by your favour [*Looks up to the windows*] Mistress What-you call-'em —pr'ythee look out now a little, and see how I'll fight for thee.

Fred. Come, sir, are you ready ?

John. O lord, sir, your servant.   [*Fight.*

Enter DUKE *and* PETRUCHIO.

Petr. What's here, fighting ? Let's part 'em. How ! Don Frederick against Don John ! How came you to fall out, gentlemen ? What's the cause?

Fred. Why, sir, it is your quarrel, and not mine, that drew this on me: I saw him lock Constantia up into that house, and I desired to wait upon her to you ; that's the cause.

Duke. O, it may be he designed to lay the obligation upon us himself, sir. We are beholden to you for this favour beyond all possibility of——

John. Pray, sir, do not throw away your thanks before you know whether I have deserved them or no. Oh, is that your design ? Sir, you must not go in there.   [Petruchio's *going to the door.*

Petr. How, sir ! not go in ?

John. No, sir, most certainly not go in.

Petr. She's my sister, and I will speak with her.

John. If she were your mother, sir, you should not, tho' it were but to ask your blessing.

Petr. Since you are so positive I'll try.

John. You shall find me a man of my word, sir.

                           [*Fight.*

Duke. Nay, pray gentlemen hold, let me compose this matter. Why do you make a scruple of letting us see Constantia?

John. Why, sir, 'twould turn a man's head round to hear these fellows talk so; there is not one word true of all that he has said.

Duke. Then you do not know where Constantia is?

John. Not I, by heavens.

Fred. O monstrous impudence! Upon my life, sir, I saw him shut her up into that house, and know his temper so, that if I had not stopped him, I dare swear by this time he would have ravished her.

John. Now that is two lies; for first, he did not see her; and next, the lady I led in, is not to be ravished, she is so willing.

Duke. But look ye, sir, this doubt may easily be cleared; let either Petruchio or I but see her, and if she be not Constantia, we engage our honours (tho' we should know her) never to discover who she is.

John. Ay, but there's the point now that I can never consent to.

Duke. Why?

John. Because I gave her my word to the contrary.

Duke. And did you never break your word with a woman.

John. Never before I lay with her; and that's the case now.

Petr. Pish, I won't be kept off thus any longer:
sir, either let me enter or I'll force my way.

Fred. No, pray sir, let that be my office: I will be
revenged on him for having betrayed me to his
friendship. [Pet. *and* Fred. *offer to fight with* John.

Duke. Nay, ye shall not offer him foul play neither.
Hold, brother, pray a word; and with you too, sir.

John. Pox on't, would they would make an end of
this business, that I might be with her again. Hark
ye, gentlemen, I'll make ye a fair proposition, leave
off this ceremony among yourselves, and those dismal
threats against me; filip up cross or pile who shall
begin first, and I'll do the best I can to entertain you
all one after another.

Enter ANTONIO.

Ant. Now do my fingers itch to be about some-
body's ears for the loss of my gold. Ha! what's here
to do, swords drawn? I must make one, tho' it cost
me the singing of ten John Dorio's more. Courage,
brave boy, I'll stand by thee as long as this tool here
lasts: and it was once a good one.

Petr. Who's this? Antonio! O, sir, you are welcome, you shall be even judge between us.

Ant. No, no, no, not I, sir, I thank ye; I'll make
work for others to judge of, I'm resolved to fight.

Petr. But we won't fight with you.

Ant. Then put up your swords, or by this hand I'll
lay about me.

John. Well said, old Bilboa, i'faith.

                [*They put up their swords.*

Petr. Pray hear us, tho': this gentleman saw him lock up my sister into that house, and he refuses to let us see her.

Ant. How, friend, is this true?

John. Nay, good sir, let not our friendship be broken before it is well made. Look ye, gentlemen, to shew ye that you are all mistaken, and that my formal friend there is an ass———

Fred. I thank you, sir.

John. I'll give you my consent that this gentleman here shall see her, if his information can satisfy you.

Duke. Yes, yes; he knows her very well.

John. Then, sir, go in here, if you please: I dare trust him with her, for he is too old to do her either good or harm.

Fred. I wonder how my gentleman will get off from all this.

John. I shall be even with you, sir, another time, for all your grinning.

Enter a Servant.

How now? Where is he?

Ser. He's run out of the back-door, sir.

John. How so?

Ser. Why, sir, he's run after the gentlewoman you brought in.

John. 'Sdeath, how durst you let her out?

Ser. Why, sir, I knew nothing.

H iij

John. No, thou ignorant rascal, and therefore I'll beat something into thee.   *[Beats him.*

Fred. What, you won't kill him?

John. Nay, come not near me, for if thou dost, by heavens, I'll give thee as much; and would do so however, but that I won't lose time from looking after my dear sweet——a pox confound you all.

   [Goes in, and shuts the door after him.

Duke. What, he has shut the door!

Fred. It's no matter, I'll lead you to a private back way, by that corner, where we shall meet him.

       [Exeunt.

ACT V. SCENE I.

Enter ANTONIO's *Servant, Constable and Officers.*

Servant.

A YOUNG woman, say'st thou, and her mother?

Man. Yes, just now come to the house; not an hour ago.

Ser. It must be they: here, friend, here's money for you; be sure you take 'em, and I'll reward you better when you have done.

Const. But, neighbour, ho——hup——shall I now —hup——know these parties? for I would——hup ——execute my office——hup——like——hup——a sober person.

Man. That's hard; but you may easily know the mother, for she is——hup——drunk.

Const. Nay——hup——if she be drunk, let—hup
——me alone to maul her ; for——hup——I abhor
a drunkard——hup——let it be man, woman, or——
hup——child.

Man. Ay, neighbour, one may see you hate drink-
ing indeed.

Const. Why, neighbour——hup——did you ever
see me drunk ? Answer me that question : did you
ever——hup——see me drunk ?

Man. No, never, never ; come away, here's the
house.   *[Exeunt.*

Enter 1st. CONSTANTIA.

Con. Oh, whither shall I run to hide myself : the
constable has seized the landlady, and I am afraid the
poor child too. How to return to Don Frederick's
house, I know not ; and if I knew, I durst not, after
those things the landlady has told me of him. If I
get not from this drunken rabble, I expose my honour ; and if I fall into my brother's hands, I lose
my life : you powers above, look down and help me :
I am faulty I confess, but greater faults have often
met with lighter punishments.

Then let not heavier yet on me be laid ;
Be what I will, I'm still what you have made.

Enter Don JOHN.

John. I'm almost dead with running, and will be
so quite, but I will overtake her.

Con. Hold, Don John, hold.

John. Who's that? ha! is it you, my dear?

Con. For heaven's sake, sir, carry me from hence, or I'm utterly undone.

John. Phoo, pox, this is the other: now could I almost beat her, for but making me the proposition. Madam, there are some a coming, that will do it a great deal better; but I am in such haste, that I vow to gad, madam——

Con. Nay, pray sir, stay, you are concerned in this as well as I; for your woman is taken.

John. Ha! my woman?   [*Goes back to her.* I vow to gad, madam, I do so highly honour your ladyship, that I would venture my life a thousand times to do you service. But pray where is she?

Con. Why, sir, she is taken by the constable.

John. Constable! Which way went he?   [*Rashly.*

Con. I cannot tell, for I run out into the streets just as he had seized upon your landlady.

John. Plague o' my landlady, I meant t'other woman.

Con. Other woman, sir! I have seen no other woman, never since I left your house!

John. S'heart, what have I been doing here then all this while? Madam, your most humble——

Con. Good sir, be not so cruel, as to leave me in this distress.

John. No, no, no, I'm only going a little way, and will be back again presently.

Con. But pray, sir, hear me, I'm in that danger—

John. No, no, no; I vow to gad, madam, no danger i'th' world. Let me alone, I warrant you. [*Exit.*

Con. He's gone, and I a lost, wretched, miserable creature, for ever.

Enter ANTONIO.

Ant. O, there she is.

Con. Who's this? Antonio! the fiercest enemy I have.

Ant. Are ye so nimble footed, gentlewoman? If I don't overtake you for all this, it shall go hard——

She'll break my wind, with a pox to her:

A plague confound all whores!   [*Exit.*

Enter Mother to the 2d CONSTANTIA, *and Kinswoman.*

Kins. But, madam, be not so angry; perhaps she'll come again.

Moth. O kinswoman, never speak of her more; for she's an odious creature to leave me thus i'th' lurch. I that have given her all her breeding, and instructed her with my own principles of education.

Kins. I protest, madam, I think she's a person that knows as much of all that as——

Moth. Knows, kinswoman! there's ne'er a woman in Italy, of thrice her years, knows so much the procedures of a true gallantry; and the infallible principles of an honourable friendship, as she does.

Kins. And therefore, madam, you ought to love her.

Moth. No, fie upon her, nothing at all, as I am a christian. When once a person fails in fundamentals,

she's at a period with me.   Besides, with all her wit,
Constantia is but a fool, and calls all the *mignarderies*
of a *bonne mien*, affectation.

Kins. Indeed, I must confess, she's given a little
too much to the careless way.

Moth. Ay, there you have hit it, kinswoman; the
careless way has quite undone her.   Will ye believe
me, kinswoman ? as I am a christian, I never could
make her do this, nor carry her body thus, but just·
when my eye was upon her ; as soon as ever my back
was turned, whip her elbows were quite out again :
would not you strange now at this ?

Kins. Bless me, sweet goodness ! But pray, madam,
how came Constantia to fall out with your ladyship ?
Did she take any thing ill of you ?

Moth. As I am a christian I can't resolve you, unless it were that I led the dance first; but for that
she must excuse me; I know she dances well, but
there are others who perhaps understand the right
swim of it as well as she :

Enter *Don* FREDERICK.

And tho' I love Constantia——

Fred. How's this ? Constantia !

Moth. I know no reason why I should be debarred
the privilege of shewing my own parts too sometimes.

Fred. If I am not mistaken, that other woman is
she Don John and I were directed to, when we came
first to town, to bring us acquainted with Constantia.

I'll try to get some intelligence from her. Pray, lady, have I never seen you before?

Kins. Yes, sir, I think you have, with another stranger, a friend of yours, one day as I was coming out of the church.

Fred. I am right then. And pray who were you talking of?

Moth. Why, sir, of an inconsiderate inconsiderable person, that has at once both forfeited the honour of my concern, and the concern of her own honour.

Fred. Very fine indeed! and is all this intended for the beautiful Constantia?

Moth. O fie upon her, sir! an odious creature, as I'm a christian, no beauty at all.

Fred. Why, does not your ladyship think her handsome?

Moth. Seriously, sir, I don't think she's ugly; but as I'm a christian, my position is, that no true beauty can be lodged in that creature, who is not in some measure buoy'd up with a just sense of what is incumbent to the devoir of a person of quality.

Fred. That position, madam, is a little severe: but however she has been incumbent formerly, as your ladyship is pleased to say; now that she's marry'd, and her husband owns the child, she is sufficiently justified for all she has done.

Moth. Sir, I must blushingly beg leave to say you are there in an error. I know there has been passages of love between 'em, but with a temperament so innocent and so refined, as it did impose a negative upon the very possibility of her being with child.

Fred. Sure, she is not well acquainted with her. Pray, madam, how long have you known Constantia?

Moth. Long enough, I think, sir, for I had the good fortune, or rather the ill one, to help her first to the light of the world.

Fred. Now cannot I discover by the fineness of this dialect, whether she be the mother or the midwife: I had better ask t'other woman.

Moth. No, sir, I assure ye, my daughter Constantia has never had a child: a child! ha, ha, ha! O goodness save us, a child!

Fred. O, then she is the mother, and it seems is not informed of the matter. Well, madam, I shall not dispute this with you any further; but give me leave to wait upon your daughter; for her friend, I assure ye, is in great impatience to see her.

Moth. Friend, sir, I know none she has. I'm sure she loaths the very sight of him.

Fred. Of whom?

Moth. Why, of Antonio, sir, he that you were pleased to say had got my daughter with child, sir; ha, ha, ha!

Fred. Still worse and worse. 'Slife! cannot she be content with not letting me understand her; but must also resolve obstinately not to understand me, because I speak plain? Why, madam, I cannot express myself your way, therefore be not offended at me for it. I tell you I do not know Antonio, nor never named him to you? I told you that the duke has owned Constantia for his wife, that her brother and he are friends, and are both now in search after her.

Moth. Then as I'm a christian, I suspect we have both been equally involved in the misfortune of a mistake. Sir, I am in the dernier confusion to avow, that tho' my daughter Constantia has been liable to several addresses; yet she never has had the honour to be produced to his grace.

Fred. So then you put her to bed to——

Moth. Antonio, sir, one whom my ebb of fortune forced me to enter into a negociation with, in reference to my daughter's person; but as I'm a christian, with that candour in the action, as I was in no kind denied to be a witness of the thing.

Fred. So now the thing is out. This is a damn'd bawd, and I as damn'd a rogue for what I did to Don John; for o' my conscience, this is that Constantia the fellow told me of. I'll make him amends, whate'er it cost me. Lady, you must give me leave not to part with you, till you meet with your daughter, for some reasons I shall tell you hereafter.

Moth. Sir, I am so highly your obligee for the manner of your enquiries, and you have grounded your determinations upon so just a basis, that I shall not be ashamed to own myself a votary to all your commands. [*Exeunt.*

Enter 2d CONSTANTIA.

2d Con. So, I'm once more freed from Antonio : but

I

whither to go now, that's the question: nothing troubles me, but that he was sent up by that young fellow, for I liked him with my soul, would he had liked me so too.

      Enter Don JOHN, *and a Shop-keeper.*

John. Which way went she?

Shop. Who?

John. The woman.

Shop. What woman?

John. Why, a young woman, a handsome woman, the handsomest woman thou ever saw'st in thy life; speak quickly, sirrah, or thou shalt speak no more.

Shop. Why, yonder's a woman: what a devil ails this fellow.   [*Exit.*

John. O my dear soul, take pity on me, and give me comfort; for I'm e'en dead for want of thee.

2d Con. O you're a fine gentleman indeed, to shut me up in your house, and send another man to me.

John. Pray hear me.

2d Con. No, I will never hear you more after such an injury: what would ye have done, if I had been kind to ye, that could use me thus before?

John. By my troth that's shrewdly urg'd.

2d Con. Besides, you basely broke your word.

John. But will you hear nothing? nor did you hear nothing? I had three men upon me at once, and had I not consented to let that old fellow up, who came to my rescue, they had all broken in whether I would or no.

2d Con. Faith it may be it was so, for I remember I heard a noise ; but suppose it was not so, what then ? Why then I'll love him however. Hark ye, sir, I ought now to use you very scurvily. But I can't find in my heart to do it.

John. Then God's blessing on thy heart for it.

2d Con. But a——

John. What ?

2d Con. I would fain—

John. Ay, so would I: come let's go.

2d Con. I would fain know, whether you can be kind to me ?

John. That thou shalt presently. Come away.

2d Con. And will you always ?

John. Always! I can't say so: but I will as often as I can.

2d Con. Phoo! I mean love me.

John. Well, I mean that too.

2d Con. Swear then.

John. That I will upon my knees. What shall I say ?

2d Con. Nay, use what words you please, so they be but hearty, and not those that are spoken by the priest, for that charm seldom proves fortunate.

John. I swear then by thy fair self, that lookest so like a deity, and art the only thing I now can think of, that I'll adore thee to my dying day.

2d Con. And here I'll vow, the minute thou dost leave me, I'll leave the world; that is, kill myself.

John. O my dear heavenly creature!—[*Kisses her.*]

That kiss now has almost put me into a swoon. For Heaven's sake, let's quickly out of the streets for fear of another scuffle. I durst encounter a whole army for thy sake, but yet methinks I had better try my courage another way; what thinkst thou?

2d Con. Well, well; why don't you then?

[*As they are going out, enter* 1st Constantia, *and just then* Antonio *seizes upon her.*

John. Who's this my old new friend has got there!

Ant. O! have I caught you gentlewoman, at last? Come, give me my gold.

Con. I hope he takes me for another, I won't answer; for I had rather he should take me for any one than who I am.

John. Pray, sir, who is that you have there by the hand?

Ant. A person of honour, sir, that has broke open my trunks, and run away with all my gold; yet I'll hold ten pounds I'll have it whipped out of her again.

2d Con. Done, I'll hold you ten pounds of that now.

Ant. Ha! by my troth you have reason; and, lady, I ask your pardon. But I'll have it whipped out of you, then, gossip.

John. Hold, sir, 'you must not meddle with my goods.

Ant. Your goods! how came she to be yours? I'm sure I bought her of her mother for five hundred good pieces of gold, and she was a-bed with me all night too. Deny that, if you dare.

2d Con. Well, and what did you do when I was a-bed with you all night? Confess that, if you dare.

Ant. Umph! say you so?

Con. I'll try if this lady will help me, for I know not whither else to go.

Ant. I shall be ashamed I see utterly, except I make her hold her peace. Pray, sir, by your leave, I hope you will allow me the speech of one word with your goods here, as you call her: 'tis but a small request.

John. Ay, sir, with all my heart. How, Constantia! madam, now you have seen that lady, I hope you will pardon the haste you met me in a little while ago; if I committed a fault you must thank her for it.

Con. Sir, if you will for her sake be persuaded to protect me from the violence of my brother, I shall have reason to thank you both.

John. Nay, madam, now that I am in my wits again, and my heart's at ease, it shall go very hard, but I will see yours so too. I was before distracted, and 'tis not strange the love of her should hinder me from remembering what was due to you, since it made me forget myself.

Con. Sir, I do know too well the power of love, by my own experience, not to pardon all the effects of it in another.

Ant. Well then, I promise you, if you will but help me to my gold again (I mean that which you and your mother stole out of my trunk) that I'll never trouble you more.

2d Con. A match; and 'tis the best that you and I could ever make.

John. Pray, madam, fear nothing; by my love I'll stand by you, and see that your brother shall do you no harm.

2d Con. Hark ye, sir, a word; how dare you talk of love, or standing by any lady but me, sir?

·*John.* By my troth that was a fault; but I did not mean in your way, I meant it only civilly.

2d Con. Ay, but if you are so very civil a gentleman, we shall not be long friends. I scorn to share your love with any one, whatsoever: and for my part I'm resolved either to have all or nothing.

John. Well, my dear little rogue, thou shalt have it all presently, as soon as we can but get rid of this company.

2d Con. Phoo! ye are always abusing me

Enter FREDERICK *and Mother.*

Fred. Come, now, madam, let not us speak one word more, but go quietly about our business, not but that I think it the greatest pleasure in the world to hear you talk, but——

Moth. Do you indeed, sir? I swear then good wits jump, sir; for I have thought so myself a very great while.

Fred. You've all the reason imaginable. O, Don John, I ask thy pardon, but I hope I shall make thee amends, for I have found out the mother, and she has promised me to help thee to thy mistress again.

John. Sir, you may save your labour, the business is done, and I am fully satisfied.

Fred. And dost thou know who she is?

John. No faith, I never ask'd her name.

Fred. Why then, I'll make thee yet more satisfied; this lady here is that very Constantia——

John. Ha! thou hast not a mind to be knocked o'er the pate too, hast thou?

Fred. No, sir, nor dare you do it neither: but for certain this is that very self-same Constantia that thou and I so long looked after.

John. I thought she was something more than ordinary; but shall I tell thee now a stranger thing than all this?

Fred. What's that?

John. Why, I will never more touch any other woman for her sake.

Fred. Well, I submit; that indeed is stranger.

2d Con. Come, mother, deliver your purse; I have delivered myself up to this young fellow, and the bargain's made with that old fellow, so he may have his gold again, that all shall be well.

Moth. As I'm a Christian, sir, I took it away only to have the honour of restoring it again; for my hard fate having not bestowed upon me a fund which might capacitate me to make you presents of my own, I had no way left for the exercise of my generosity but by putting myself into a condition of giving back what was yours.

Ant. A very generous design indeed! So now, I'll

1

e'en turn a sober person, and leave off this wenching, and this fighting, for I begin to find it does not agree with me.

Fred. Madam, I'm heartily glad to meet your ladyship here; we have been in a very great disorder since we saw you. What's here, our landlady and the child again!

Enter DUKE, PETRUCHIO, *and Landlady with the Child.*

Petr. Yes, we met her going to be whipped, in a drunken constable's hands that took her for another.

John. Why then, pray let her e'en be taken and whipped for herself, for on my word she deserves it.

Land. Yes, I'm sure of your good word at any time.

Con. Hark ye, dear landlady.

Land. O, sweet goddess! is it you? I have been in such a peck of troubles since I saw you; they took me, and they tumbled me, and they hauled me, and they pulled me, and they called me painted Jezable, and the poor little babe here did so take on. Come hither, my lord, come hither: here is Constantia.

Con. For Heaven's sake peace; yonder is my brother, and if he discovers me, I'm certainly ruined.

Duke. No, madam, there is no danger.

Con. Were there a thousand dangers in those arms, I would run thus to meet them.

Duke. O, my dear, it were not safe that any should

be here at present; for now my heart is so o'er-pressed with joy, that I should scarce be able to de-fend thee.

Petr. Sister, I'm so asham'd of all the faults, which my mistake has made me guilty of, that I know not how to ask your pardon for them.

Con. No, brother, the fault was mine, in mistaking you so much, as not to impart the whole truth to you at first; but having begun my love without your consent, I never durst acquaint you with the progress of it.

Duke. Come, let the consummation of our present joys blot out the memory of all these past mistakes.

John. And when shall we consummate our joys?

2d Con. Never:
We'll find out ways shall make them last for ever.

John. Now see the odds, 'twixt married folks and
friends:
Our love begins just where their passion ends.

[*Exeunt.*

EPILOGUE.

PERHAPS you, gentlemen, expect to-day,
The author of this fag-end of a play,
According to the modern way of wit,
Should strive to be before-hand with the Pit ;
Begin to rail at you, and subtly too,
Prevent th' affront by giving the first blow.
He wants not precedents, which often sway,
In matters far more weighty than a play :
But he, no grave admirer of a rule,
Won't by example learn to play the fool.
The end of plays should be to entertain,
And not to keep the auditors in pain.
Giving our price, and for what trash we please,
He thinks the play being done, you should have ease.
No wit, no sense, no freedom, and a box,
Is much like paying money for the stocks.
Besides, the author dreads the strut and mein
Of new-prais'd poets, having often seen
Some of his fellows, who have writ before,
When Nel has danc'd her jig, steal to the door,
Hear the Pit clap, and with conceit of that,
Swell, and believe themselves the lord knows what.
Most writers, now-a-days, are grown so vain,
That once approv'd, they write, and write again,

Till they have writ away the fame they got.
Our friend this way of writing fancies not,
And hopes you will not tempt him with your praise,
To rank himself with some that write new plays :
For he knows ways enough to be undone,
Without the help of poetry for one.

Printed in Great Britain
by Amazon.co.uk, Ltd.,
Marston Gate.